TOMORROW'S WORLD: **COMPUTERS**
THE NEXT GENERATION

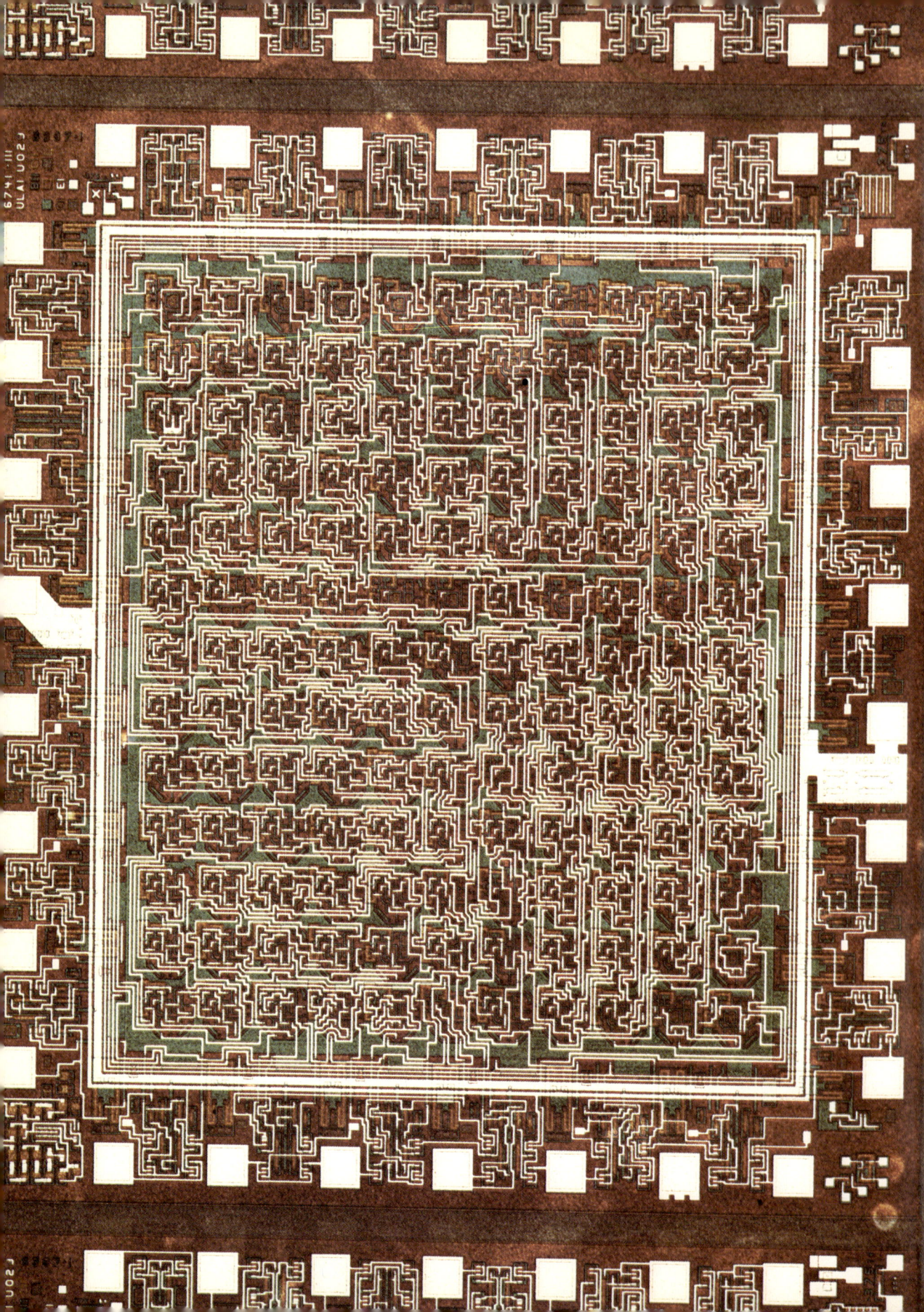

TOMORROW'S WORLD
Computers

Jack Weber

ARCO PUBLISHING, INC.
New York

For Kay

The author would like to thank all the companies mentioned for their co-operation and help during the writing of this book.

Tomorrow's World was first broadcast on British television in 1965 and has been screened every year since then.

Published 1985 by Arco Publishing, Inc.
215 Park Avenue South, New York, NY 10003

© The British Broadcasting Corporation 1984

All rights reserved. No part of this book may be reproduced, by any means, without permission in writing from the publisher, except by a reviewer who wishes to quote brief excerpts in connection with a review in a magazine or newspaper.

Library of Congress Cataloging in Publication Data

Weber, Jack, 1950-
   Computers, the next generation.

   (Tomorrow's world)
   Includes index.
   1. Supercomputers. 2. Parallel processing (Electronic computers). 3. Artificial intelligence. I. Title.
QA76.5.W387   1985   001.64   84-16744
ISBN 0-668-06339-4

Printed in Italy

FRONTISPIECE The urban landscape of the silicon city. This chip is about 3mm. across *(see* CHAPTER SIX*).*

TITLE PAGE Computers help to design the chips which will go to make new computers *(see* CHAPTER SIX*).*

Contents

7 **CHAPTER ONE**
Changing Expectations

23 **CHAPTER TWO**
The Next Generation

41 **CHAPTER THREE**
Modern Architecture

53 **CHAPTER FOUR**
Thinkchips

71 **CHAPTER FIVE**
Face to Interface

87 **CHAPTER SIX**
Silicon Cities

105 **CHAPTER SEVEN**
Beyond the Silicon Chip

121 **CHAPTER EIGHT**
The Limits

126 **ILLUSTRATION SOURCES**
127 **FURTHER READING**
127 **INDEX**

CHAPTER ONE
Changing Expectations

No more than six computers will ever be sold in the commercial market.
                                                        Howard Aiken, 1950

Predicting the future of the computer revolution has always been a tricky business. The irony of Howard Aiken's prophecy is that he was the man who designed IBM's first-ever computer. Today IBM is the largest manufacturing company in the world with a turnover that is larger than the income of many countries. Yet Aiken was not alone in his views; Alan Turing, an outstanding genius who laid the foundations of modern computer theory back in the 1930s, believed that just three machines would satisfy all of Britain's computing needs.

Of course, it is very easy and quite unfair to look with hindsight on the astonishing growth of computers (over a million are bought in Britain every year) and laugh at such predictions. Actually Aiken and Turing made very sensible predictions about computers as they saw them. What let them down was that computers changed their character; they became seen as something different and so the predictions were no longer relevant.

Today we are facing a new computer revolution at least as big as that first one. Once again the change will be a radical one, not just a matter of smaller, cheaper, faster computers, but different computers. If our predictions are to be of any value we need to look carefully at how computers have been changing.

Great expectations

Howard Aiken worked as a research physicist at Harvard University. Frustrated by the vast amounts of tedious calculation needed for his work, he began to consider the possibility of automating the mathematical drudgery. Adding machines already existed but they were too limited; what he wanted was a general-purpose calculator that could be fed with numbers, told how to solve the calculation and left to produce an answer. In 1939 he took his proposal to International Business Machines, already a highly successful company producing typewriters, adding machines and punched-card equipment. The company quickly reached a decision: Aiken was to get a million dollars and the full backing of IBM's technical facilities. Over the next four years a gleaming monster was produced. Encased in stainless steel and glass, it was 8 feet high and over 50 feet long, a rotating shaft ran its full length and from its depths came a continuous clattering 'like a roomful of old ladies knitting away with steel needles'. Its abilities were truly prodigious; it could remember 72 numbers at a time and do three additions every second. Officially it was called the Automatic Sequence Controlled Calculator, known to its friends as the Harvard Mark 1, but in the public mind it soon became the 'electronic brain'.

Aiken's aim had been to automate the drudgery of scientific calculation, and he had achieved it. But how many people could reasonably be

ABOVE Howard Aiken

OPPOSITE Enormously magnified, this is the intricate detail of an array of gates on a silicon chip

The Harvard Mark 1. Completed in 1943, it worked almost continuously for fifteen years

expected to need such a machine? At most a few of the wealthiest and most advanced universities and, of course, the military (from the very beginning the Harvard Mark 1 had been assigned to ballistics calculations for the US Navy). From that point of view six sales was quite a reasonable estimate. Why, then, did things turn out so differently?

When the Harvard Mark 1 was installed, the first warning signs were already coming into view: just two years later, in 1946, a new computer, called ENIAC, was performing 5000 additions a second. Ever since then it has been an inescapable fact of computer life that anything you make is obsolete by the time it is built. ENIAC suffered the same fate with the arrival of the stored-program computer, which we shall be meeting again later. But at the same time another, even more profound change was taking place and it was happening in the unlikely setting of the Lyons Teashop Company.

Lyons Teashops were a very successful chain of London restaurants. The company was blessed with a progressive management who had the vision to see that computers need not be confined to scientific calculation but could as easily be adapted to accounting, inventory and other business activities. Unable to buy the sort of computer the company would need, Lyons set up a team to build its own. It was called LEO, the Lyons Electronics Office, and it went on to become one of the most successful commercial computers of its time.

What Lyons had done was to introduce data processing and in so doing had liberated the computer from its role as a glorified calculator. Six sales was no longer a realistic assessment.

The change that took place with LEO was a change of expectation; today, at least, we should be familiar with such changes. The information revolution is altering the ways in which we read words, view

LEFT A small fraction of the 18,000 electronic valves which made ENIAC the most complex electronic system of its time

RIGHT Lyons Coventry Street Corner House in the 1950s. Lyons teashops were one of the first businesses to become computerised

pictures and learn facts. The microchip has put computers into our washing machines, our cars and our pockets. We take for granted that banking and shopping are changing rapidly as money becomes electronic. All these are familiar novelties and can no longer surprise us. But what about the computer chip that is designed to be surgically implanted into the spine so as to connect directly with the body's central nervous system? Do we know what to expect of that? How about artificial intelligence, expert systems, computers made of plastic and computers that are, quite literally, alive?

These are the sorts of projects that computer research is currently involved in. There are many others, which may sound just as unlikely; together they form the subject of this book. We shall look at how they work, see how they could be used and try to predict (that tricky business) what part they will play in our future experience of computers.

General-purpose machines

Computers have got to where they are today (which is almost everywhere) because of one essential quality they all share: they are general-purpose machines. This fact makes computers quite unlike any other technological product.

Machines such as lathes, video recorders, combine harvesters and pocket calculators have all been designed to do one particular job, and that job is the only one that they are able to perform. Computers, however, are not like that. The computer that produces images in a brain scanner could also be used to play a video game, or it could be programmed to do a company's accounts. The reason for all this versatility is that computers handle the one thing that is common to every activity that there is – information.

ABOVE Joseph Marie Jacquard, the French silk weaver whose loom was the forerunner of later punched card equipment used in computing

LEFT The Jacquard loom

We are used to thinking of information as something to be found in books, something that we may know or need to find out. But it may not be immediately obvious that information is also a part of doing things. In fact the idea has been around for quite some time. It was used to particularly good effect in the late eighteenth century by the French silk weavers of Lyon: especially by Joseph-Marie Jacquard (1752-1834).

Jacquard wanted some way of speeding up the weaving, in particular the tedious process of setting and resetting the threads at every throw of the shuttle. If the pattern was at all complicated this became a very demanding task and often led to mistakes. Building on the earlier ideas

ABOVE Charles Babbage

RIGHT Computers need not be electronic – Charles Babbage's Analytical Engine was designed as a fully programmable steam powered computer. Unfortunately engineering difficulties prevented its completion, this part is virtually all that was built

Ada, Countess of Lovelace. Friend and supporter of Charles Babbage, she was a talented mathematician and a pioneer of computer programming. She was the only child of Lord Byron's brief marriage

of other weavers, Jacquard created a mechanical system for controlling the threads, using punched cards to represent every step of the design. The cards, as many as several thousand joined end to end in a great concertina, were fed through the machine. As each one moved into position its pattern of holes would allow through or hold back different combinations of rods which carried the threads. Straight away weaving became faster and more accurate.

Jacquard's contribution to industrial productivity was rewarded by a state pension and the Légion d'honneur. But, unknowingly, he had made a far greater contribution to the birth of computing. The Jacquard loom separated out for the first time the information content of an intricate task. The loom handled the threads, while the cards handled the pattern which was pure information.

Jacquard's loom was by no stretch of the imagination a computer; it was, after all, a specialized machine that could do only the one job of weaving. But it opened the way to what was to come.

A few years later Charles Babbage (1792-1871), an English mathematician, invented the computer and his collaborator, Ada, Countess of Lovelace, began to lay the foundations of our modern understanding of these new machines. She wrote of Babbage's design for an 'analytical engine' that it 'weaves algebraical patterns just as the Jacquard loom weaves flowers and leaves'.

The Ford Probe IV – an experimental car which, among other things, uses its computer to vary the body shape so as to make it more aerodynamic at high speeds

The first production car with computer controlled suspension. This Lotus Esprit uses its computer to operate hydraulic rams on each of the wheels, allowing a perfectly smooth ride over almost any road surface. The computer can also be instructed to vary the feel of the suspension in any way desired

A typical car computer. The unit marked CPU is the microprocessor, the ROM next to it is the memory which contains all the stored information about the engine's performance. In one minute of driving it performs as many calculations as would take a person with a hand calculator forty-five years to do

Patterns of information

Today we can see such patterns wherever there is a computer. Look, for example, under the hood of any of the more advanced of today's cars and you can find a small computer called a microprocessor. Its job is to bring together information about various aspects of the car's performance; it then uses this information either to tell the driver what is going on or to make adjustments directly to the car.

One important function a computer can perform in a car is continuously to control the mixture of gasoline and air being fed to the cylinders. By adjusting this mixture it can ensure that the engine is always working efficiently and so keep fuel consumption to a minimum. To do this it needs access to various items of information. Some are relatively straightforward, such as the pressure of air coming into the engine, the temperature of that air and the engine speed. All the time the computer must ensure that the correct amount of air is mixed with the correct amount of fuel. If the air pressure increases, more air will be blown into the engine and so upset the balance; if the temperature drops, extra fuel must be used to maintain power; and the engine speed is important because it affects its performance. All of these measurements can be obtained from simple electrical sensors mounted in the air intake and on the distributor.

But one piece of information is more subtle and cannot be measured in this direct way. It concerns the behavior of the engine. For every combination of pressure, temperature and speed there is just one correct mixture of air and gas, and the computer needs to know what this is so that it can operate the air valve and the fuel injection valve correctly. This information is something that can only be found from careful trials on the basic engine design; it is the pattern that makes sense of all the other information. Because it cannot and does not need to be measured all the time, it is stored within the computer like a table of numbers or a mathematical formula.

Combining all this information the computer raises and lowers the air supply, increases and decreases the fuel injection, constantly weaving a complex pattern of changing mixtures. How, though, is this different from Jacquard's loom? It is more complex certainly, but why is one a computer and not the other? The reason is that the microprocessor in the car is not tied to that particular task. The same microprocessor can be used in different models of car or in a truck perhaps. It could be taken right out of the car and used in an automatic weather station, for example, where readings of temperature, air pressure and the speed of an anemometer need to be recorded. Connected up to different sensors it could operate a patient's life support system in a hospital.

The success of such simple computers has been quite astonishing. Today, one of the largest computer manufacturers in the world, in terms of numbers produced, is not a computer company at all but General Motors. This organization has the capacity to make 25,000 microprocessors a day, all of them destined to go into cars. Within a few years production cars will have computer-controlled dynamic suspension, using information from sensors on each wheel to give an absolutely even ride over any surface (a technique some racing cars already use). Brakes will operate under computer supervision so that unequal wear will never again cause sideways pull, and the computer will detect and prevent a locked-wheel skid before the driver has even noticed it. Looking beyond that, computer navigation and computer guidance are already on the drawing board. Manipulating information is clearly a very powerful ability, but success depends on finding the best way of doing it.

The first draft
When the silk weavers of Lyon developed punched-card systems for their looms, they were handling information in a strict sequence: it was very important that they should do so if the required pattern of cloth was to emerge. Similarly, when Howard Aiken built the Harvard Mark 1, he put his instructions for each calculation onto a roll of punched paper. This was moved past a row of detectors which, like the rods in Jacquard's loom, responded to the pattern of holes at every step. In this way instructions were given to the machine in the correct predetermined order, hence the machine's official name: the Automatic Sequence Controlled Calculator. This list of instructions was what we now call a program and the Harvard Mark 1 was the world's first fully operational program-controlled computer.

Its sequential approach was fine for dealing with operations that could be planned out in advance and needed to be followed through in a strict order. But this is rarely possible in the jobs computers now do. The car computer, for instance, has a great many tasks to perform. Some of these are continuous activities, others only need to be done in response to an unpredictable fault or an instruction from the driver. Supplying lists of commands on paper tape or punched cards, or even a more modern medium like magnetic tape, could never be fast enough or flexible enough to cope with this.

The solution of this problem was the single most important step in the practical development of the modern computer. The man who gets the credit for it is John von Neumann (1903-1957).

Von Neumann was a Hungarian-American mathematician who worked at the Institute for Advanced Study in Princeton, New Jersey. In the early 1930s he had made an important contribution to theoretical physics through his work on quantum mechanics. With the coming of the Second World War he was appointed mathematical consultant to the secret Manhattan Project which was developing the atom bomb. The number of calculations involved was simply enormous and, like Howard Aiken before him, von Neumann felt the need for some means of speeding up the work. At the same time another secret project was being

John von Neumann whose pioneering work created the basis for much of modern computing

ENIAC in February 1946. The man in uniform on the right is Herman Goldstine, the army officer whose meeting with John von Neumann prompted the writing of the First Draft

undertaken by the US Army Ordnance Department, which was building the Electronic Numerical Integrator and Calculator (ENIAC) to produce ballistics tables for new guns and rockets. In the summer of 1944 von Neumann happened to meet the army officer in charge of ENIAC, who told him about the project. Von Neumann immediately realized that it could help solve his problems at Los Alamos, but he could also see its limitations. ENIAC would be very fast but, because it was only intended to do one sequence of calculations, it was wired for just that one task. Changing the program would involve rewiring much of the machine.

In the following months von Neumann became increasingly involved in trying to produce a design of computer that would be truly versatile. He presented the answer in June 1945 in a document entitled 'First Draft of a Report on the EDVAC' (Electronic Discrete Variable Automatic Computer). It was the definitive description of what computers would be from then on.

The essential difference which von Neumann had introduced was the concept of the stored program. Instead of taking instructions from a paper tape or some other external source, the computer would store the program within its own electronic memory.

Why was this such an important development? The first advantage was speed. ENIAC was a thousand times faster than the electro-mechanical Harvard Mark 1 because it used vacuum tubes, which could switch on and off very rapidly. In the same way, replacing the mechanical paper tape system with electronic memory removed one of the computer's worst bottlenecks. But a far more important benefit was that it did away with the need for a strictly sequential style of operation.

Given a large enough memory, several different programs could be held in it at the same time and each would be instantly available whenever it was required, in whatever order. What is more, it would be very easy for one program to call up another if the need arose, building up a sequence of instructions that was determined by the outcome of previous operations rather than by sticking to a rigid list of commands. Because programs are not stored in a permanent form within the electronic memory, they could even be made to alter each other or themselves, so as to adapt to changing needs or to learn from past mistakes.

It was a very simple change and yet it lifted computers from being machines whose flexibility depended on human skill with soldering irons and paper tape to devices of such potential complexity that we are unlikely ever to exhaust their versatility. Since then virtually every computer has used the structure described in the 'First Draft'. They are known to computer scientists as 'von Neumann machines'.

So far we have touched on two premonitions of the changes that are going to affect computers and computing in the coming years. The first is the change of expectation. Computers are capable of virtually limitless flexibility but they will progress only as fast as we can understand, and feel confident about, new ways of using them. Our changing expectations, and the new applications that arise from them, form one topic of this book. The second change, intimately tied up with the first, affects the way that computers operate. After forty years of almost total domination, the von Neumann machine is now under threat. New ways of manipulating information are being devised, partly as a result of our improved understanding of how the human brain does its information handling. These form another theme. But there is one more strand that needs to be woven into this picture. It is the physical make-up of the new computer, the hardware that will make real all of these ambitions: new chips, new materials and new ways for machines and people to communicate.

Pulse patterns
Computers are able to handle information by encoding it as a pattern of electrical pulses. This is called a binary pattern because it is made up of only two elements: either a pulse is there or it is not. No half measures are allowed. Because it is so unambiguous it is a particularly convenient way to work with electronics, as this type of pattern is far less likely to be affected by problems like electrical interference or inaccuracies in the components. But the binary system is also an ideal form in which to handle information, because it allows exceedingly complex operations to be built up out of a sequence of extremely simple ones.

The two states of the binary system, pulse and no pulse, are usually written as '1' and '0'. A typical pattern may then look like this: 01001110. Each '0' and '1' is called a bit and, because there are 8 of them in this case, the overall pattern is known as an 8-bit word; many microcomputers use 8-bit words, but larger computers employ words of 32 bits or even more. However, these are not words as we normally think of them; each pattern of bits actually represents a number (01001110 is the binary representation of 78). These binary numbers can be added, subtracted, multiplied and divided just like our familiar decimal numbers. They may appear very cumbersome to human eyes but they are ideal for computer use because, breaking the process down to its smallest steps, the computer never has to deal with anything more complex than '1' or '0', on or off, pulse or no pulse.

The circuits that manipulate these binary numbers are themselves made up of numerous simple units called gates. A typical gate has several input connections and one output. Whether or not a pulse appears on the output lead is controlled by the combination of pulses at the inputs. For example, one commonly used gate is designed so that a '0' will appear at the output only if there is a '1' at each of the inputs. If any of the inputs is '0' then the output will be '1'. Other types of gate respond differently. By combining gates together it is possible to build up circuits that can perform arithmetic, recognize specific patterns of bits, or alter these patterns according to whatever rules we wish to devise. However complex we make those rules the process always boils down to simple steps involving decisions between '0' and '1'.

An adding circuit, for example, is basically quite straightforward. It is simply a combination of gates which, if fed with the binary pattern 00111000 (which corresponds to 56) and the pattern 01110101 (which is 117) will produce an output of 10101101 (the binary form of 173). Of course, it must also give the right answer for any other pairs of numbers.

Then again, binary numbers need not necessarily represent numbers at all. We can just as easily use them as a code for letters. This book is being written on a computer keyboard with a word-processing program in the machine. Every time I type 'K' the keyboard sends the code 1001011 to the computer, which stores it as the next letter of the text. Now, 1001011 is also the number 75 but there is no confusion inside the computer because other binary patterns, operating through various gates, ensure that whenever 1001101 comes from the keyboard it is printed out as the letter K and not as a number.

On the face of it binary may appear a very inefficient means of handling data. Even a small number like 173 required 8 binary bits and the symbol K is obviously more compact than 1001011. Fortunately, computers have two essential qualities: they can store a large amount of data and they can process it very rapidly. The most advanced modern computers can do up to 100 million arithmetic operations, such as multiplying or comparing two numbers, every second. And they can store over 4 million numbers, each of them 64 bits long. If all of these 1s and 0s were typed single-spaced on ordinary A4 sheets they would form a stack of paper as high as a 19-story building. It is a far cry from the 3 additions per second and 72 stored numbers of the Harvard Mark 1.

Running faster than reality

One application that needs this sort of speed and capacity is weather forecasting. At Britain's Meteorological Office in Bracknell, Berkshire, a Cyber 205 computer takes in readings from weather stations, ships, buoys, aircraft and high-flying balloons throughout the northern hemisphere. It uses them to plot values at every intersection of a giant square grid centred on the North Pole. Fifteen such grids, representing slices through different levels of the atmosphere, result in a three-dimensional mesh of atmospheric information covering nearly half the globe. Working its way through this mesh, point by point, the computer calculates the influence of the adjacent grid points above, below and on each side. It then produces new figures to show what the conditons are likely to be at that spot twelve minutes later. When it has completed the whole of the map on all fifteen slices, it starts again, stepping the forecast forward another twelve minutes. After 120 repetitions, involving one hundred thousand million calculations, it will have produced a predicted weather pattern for 24 hours ahead. This is calculation on a heroic scale - 'number crunching' to use the jargon.

Speed is of the essence in a job like this. Any computer that took more than twelve minutes to work through the complete grid would simply be producing forecasts that were getting further and further out of date. The whole exercise is pointless unless the computer can race through it faster than reality. In fact, the Cyber 205 manages to do the full 24-hour forecast in only 4 minutes.

The one development that has made possible such high speeds and storage densities is the silicon chip. Computers could certainly have developed without chips, but they would be playing a very different role. As things are, chips are the engine that drives the computer age

OPPOSITE Weather balloons like this provide the computer with measurements at different heights in the atmosphere

BELOW LEFT The Cyber 205 computer at the Meteorological Office in Bracknell. It is one of the most powerful computers currently in use

BELOW RIGHT Once the computer has completed its prediction of weather conditions for 12 or 24 hours ahead, these plotting machines can automatically produce the charts

forward. Since the first ones appeared in the early 1960s their real cost has halved every 18 months, while the amount of circuitry that can be fitted onto each one has virtually doubled every year. No other technology has ever developed so fast.

Packing them in
Each chip starts out as pure crystalline silicon. Then, tiny amounts of other metals are introduced into it in a very precise pattern. These impurities alter the silicon's electrical properties, allowing the chip manufacturer to produce transistors and other components within the solid piece. By careful laying out of the impurity pattern in several layers through the chip, it is possible to make complete circuits containing thousands of individual gates together with their interconnections. Yet the size of a typical chip, or integrated circuit as it is also known, is only about three millimetres square and one tenth of a millimetre thick.

A silicon chip – it is the square in the centre, dwarfed by the packaging which protects it and makes it manageable

We shall return to the subject of how silicon chips are manufactured in Chapter Six and examine there the technological advances that are being made in the drive to produce ever more intricate circuitry on ever smaller pieces of silicon. But it is worth looking now at some of the reasons for this relentless pursuit of miniaturization. In the early days of computing, when a machine like ENIAC weighed 30 tons and filled a very large room, there was a clear advantage in making things smaller. Today that same sort of computing power is available in a home microcomputer which can be carried in one hand. Why then is it still so important to cut the circuitry down in size?

The reasons are complex. Partly it is to do with the economics of integrated-circuit production and partly with the way that chips work. Chips are made on circular wafers of silicon about 10 centimetres across. Each wafer costs a certain amount to produce and the 'doping' processes, which introduce the impurities, cost so much per wafer. Taken together these give a cost per wafer of processed silicon. What you choose to make out of the wafer has little effect on the cost, so the more chips that you can squeeze in, the cheaper each one becomes. Now, even though each wafer costs a lot of money it is far from perfect. Defects, bits of dirt and other blemishes are scattered over its surface. If individual chips are large they are more likely to contain one of these faults; if you can make the chips smaller the productivity goes up and so they get even cheaper.

Once you are on this path there is no turning back. Given that silicon costs so much per square millimetre it makes sense to pack more circuitry into each chip. That way you will be able to do with one chip what previously required several. In order to achieve that you need to make the impurity patterns even finer. But because of the chip's structure, every time you produce a pattern that is twice as fine you become able to pack in not twice but as much as eight times the number of components. So chips get even smaller and even cheaper.

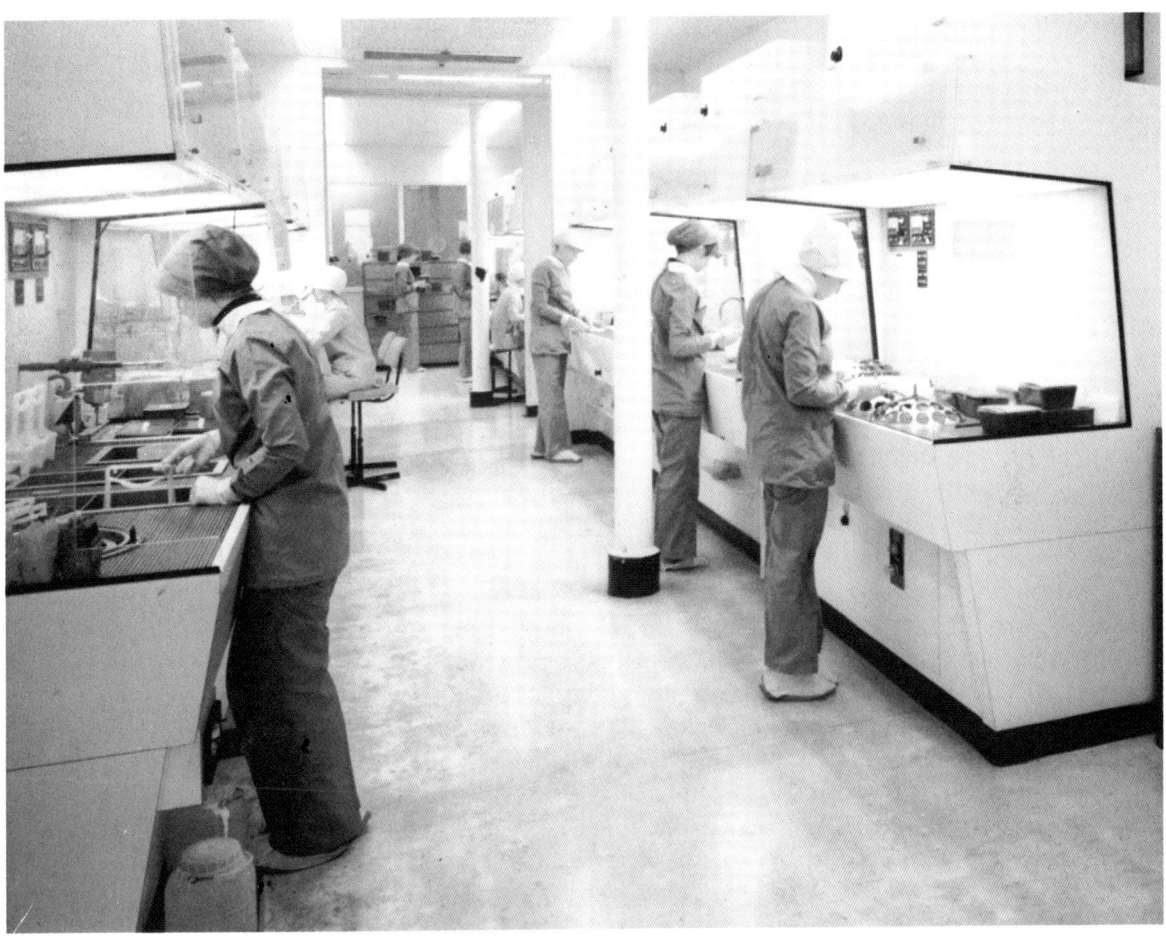

Chip manufacture – a blend of high-tech automation and human skill

All the while that this is going on you are under pressure from customers to supply chips that can handle more numbers more quickly. And what is it that makes chips slow? Size. Small gates can operate faster than large gates, small chips are faster than large chips. Small complex chips are fastest of all because they cut out the time delays which are introduced by all the wires needed to join up many simpler chips. As chips get cheaper and faster, so computers become cheaper and faster. Lower prices bring new applications and more demand. Prices fall, productivity rises, complexity multiplies. And so it goes on. In the mid-1950s a single transistor cost about four dollars; now, in the mid-1980s, four dollars will buy an integrated circuit containing some 30,000 transistors and a lot else besides.

Will it ever stop? In the final chapter we shall be looking at the limits of computing. How fast, how small and how clever can computers become before disappearing in a puff of smoke? For the present, however, there seems to be no indication that the growth of computing is slowing down. Quite the opposite in fact.

CHAPTER TWO
The Next Generation

In the summer of 1981 a bombshell arrived in the mail. Leading computer scientists in Europe and America received an invitation that was to shake the computer industry and send a shiver through governments. Angry letters were written, committees were set up, advertisements were issued to reassure shareholders. Even today it remains a prime topic of conversation wherever computer people meet.

The invitation, which came from the Japan Information Processing Development Centre, was for an international conference, to be held in Tokyo in October 1981, to discuss the fifth-generation computer. Japan, it announced, was planning to create the next generation of computers by 1992 and it wished this to be a collaborative project involving Western companies and academics. With some exceptions, the West's computer community did not see it in that light. They took it as a declaration of commercial and intellectual war.

In the United States, in particular, it has been received as the biggest blow to scientific self-respect since the Russians launched their Sputnik in 1957 and so began the space race. Computer experts spoke of having been 'sucked of information' when visiting Japan and wrote of the risks to American defence. A recent article described the situation as 'a brutal competition between the United States and Japan'. In Britain the government set up the Alvey committee, which recommended a $450 million investment to meet the challenge: its proposal was accepted, but the involvement of foreign-owned companies was forbidden unless 'it is guaranteed that valuable technical information will not leak from the United Kingdom'.

Few Western experts attended the Tokyo conference; even fewer spoke at it. There was only one contribution from Britain although a small group went to listen to the proceedings.

Whether or not these attitudes are justified, almost everyone is agreed that, in one bold stroke, the Japanese plan has defined the nature of what computers and computing will be like to the end of this century. Today there is no university computing department or major computer manufacturer that is not involved with the ideas of the fifth generation. And it is not just because of commercial competition or for reasons of national pride, but because the fifth generation plan offers a challenge that is daring, exciting and just about possible.

The aim is to produce a computer personal assistant. A machine that adapts itself to the needs of its human user rather than demanding, as present-day computers do, that we should structure our thoughts and instructions to suit the computer. It will, like any good assistant, be there not only to perform the mental drudgery but also to offer advice based on detailed knowledge of the subject. It will speak our language, whether that be English, French or Japanese. When faced with a problem, it will not ask us how to tackle it but will work out its own strategy. If requested it will, at any stage, explain its reasoning in reaching a particular conclusion or adopting a particular line of thought.

Japan already dominates the computer chip industry. The Fifth Generation project is intended to give it supremacy in computing too. Here we see Japanese employees taking a break

Information machines

What sort of machine will it be that has these qualities? We have already seen that computers have two basic characteristics: they are general-purpose machines and they handle information. We can now add another description to this list – computers are problem-solving machines. Now, problems can come in many different forms. Solving a complicated mathematical equation is clearly a problem, and having to solve a great many of them is an even bigger problem. Handling the personnel records of a large organization, so that details of any employee's salary, department, home address, tax code and so on are always available and can be updated when required, is another type of problem. Deciding on a sensible chess move is also a problem, but so is drawing the actions of a cartoon character in an animated film. Computers can do all of these things, which is why we find them useful.

Problem solving of this sort requires information and it requires a plan of action. In the examples just given the information includes such things as the mathematical formula; the relevant facts about all the employees; the present positions of all the pieces on the chessboard; the rules of chess; and the shape and colouring of the character to be drawn. There is much more besides. But what about the plan of action? If we examine in general the process of problem solving we find that there are three broad types of approach. In computing terminology they are usually called algorithmic, heuristic and knowledge-based.

Almost all present-day computer applications employ the algorithmic and heuristic techniques. One of the characteristics of the fifth generation is that it will rely very heavily on knowledge-based reasoning. So, we need to examine these three methods in a little more detail and understand the differences between them.

Imagine that you are giving someone directions on how to get somewhere. They will consist of a list of instructions something like: 'Take the second on the left, walk as far as the Post Office, then turn right and it is half a mile along on the left-hand side.' These directions are an algorithm: an ordered list of instructions specifying how a particular problem is to be solved. It breaks up the problem into individually manageable steps and usually specifies very strictly the order in which they must be carried out – turning right before taking the second on the left will clearly take you in completely the wrong direction. But the algorithm may contain sequences that need to be repeated many times and it may branch off into various alternatives such as: 'If you are coming during the week take the number 23 bus, but if it is Sunday you must walk'.

Algorithms are the commonest type of computer program. They perform mathematical calculations, they sort long lists of names into alphabetical order, they ensure that the microprocessor-controlled washing machine follows its proper sequence of steps and does not, for example, spin while still full of water. Any procedure that can be

Chess is so complex that it would take longer than the total age of the universe to find just one perfect move

unambiguously defined as a sequence of simple operations can be programmed into a computer as an algorithm.

This is very useful but it is not the answer to everything. There are some problems for which we simply do not know an algorithm and others which are just too large to be handled in such an organized way. Take again the case of giving directions. This time we are faced with a simple enough problem: a delivery van needs to call at twelve addresses and, in order to keep our fuel costs down, we wish to tell the driver which order he should visit them in so as to travel the shortest distance. The algorithm is quite simple to write: we feed it into our microcomputer and wait – but no answer will come out for a very long time. Because, for twelve addresses, there are 479,001,600 different itineraries. Even allowing for the fact that half of them can be ignored because it makes no difference which way round we go, that still leaves us with an awful lot of computing.

The same applies to chess. The rules are fairly simple and can easily be incorporated into a computer program, so can the layout of pieces on the board. But how is the machine to select its moves? A sensible approach might be to consider each possible move and countermove, selecting that which leads to the surest and quickest victory. But here too the algorithmic approach falls foul of large numbers. A typical game of chess contains around one million, million, million, million, million, million, million, million, million, million, million, million, million, million, million, million, million, million, million, million (1 followed by 120 zeroes) possible variations. Testing each of them is just not possible.

Faced with such numbers we may be forgiven for wondering how anyone ever manages to play chess or drive delivery vans without being overwhelmed by indecision. The answer seems to be that our brains have developed the ability to ignore obviously stupid possibilities without even considering them. We may not necessarily pick the very best possible choice (games of chess would be totally predictable and boring if we did), but at least we manage to narrow the field down to manageable proportions and then use common sense mixed with trial and error to make our choice. Computers have to rely on the same technique: it is called heuristic.

In fact, heuristic programs consist entirely of algorithms, but the algorithms are there not to solve the overall problem but to tackle the various smaller problems into which it has been broken down. For example in the case of the delivery van (it is always known in computing circles as the travelling salesman problem) one algorithm which may reasonably be used is to find groups of addresses that are clustered together. These, of course, should all be visited while the van is in the area rather than going elsewhere and coming back for some of them later in the journey.

These two techniques, the algorithmic and the heuristic, rely on our being able to supply some information and some rules about how it is to be manipulated. As long as the problem can be presented in this form, they are very effective: we use them as part of our own mental processes and we have applied them most successfully to computers. But they are only a part of the problem-solving armoury: their usefulness and ingenuity are undisputed, their shortcoming is that they do not know anything.

Knowledge machines

One morning you turn up at the doctor's office with a raised temperature, a sore throat and a red rash. How does the doctor proceed? By an algorithm? Heuristically? What about the financial adviser who must judge the market and select the best moment to buy or sell commodities; or the geologist who, given a great pile of field data, must take the risky decision to drill for oil or to look elsewhere. Are these people being paid high salaries for their ability to go step by step through a list of operations? No, their value lies in something much more subtle – knowledge and experience.

It is this most human of problem-solving abilities, i.e. expertise, which the computers of the fifth generation are aiming for. To achieve it they will have to go beyond the conventional reliance on information. Information is specific (this car is four years old) whereas knowledge is general (each state in the U.S. issues its own automotive license plates). Knowledge always tells us how to relate facts according to a broader scheme and how to draw conclusions from them.

The very first computer programs that tried to encapsulate some area

A doctor's expertise depends on skill and experience – these are the qualities which computing now aims to capture

of human specialist knowledge appeared in the early 1970s. They were called expert systems. Today there are thousands of expert systems being developed, and about a hundred in regular practical use. The best of them perform better than any human expert in their field.

Patient 219
Patient 219, a 42-year-old woman, was admitted to the Santa Clara Valley Medical Center in San Jose, California, showing a number of severe symptoms. Over the next few days doctors at the hospital carried out numerous tests and debated the possible diagnoses. Eventually they were able to diagnose tuberculous meningitis, a serious disease in which the bacteria responsible for causing TB infect the cerebro-spinal fluid which bathes the brain and fills the spinal cord. Anti-bacterial drugs were prescribed and, fortunately, treatment was successful.

A few miles away in Stanford, a team of doctors and computer scientists led by Dr Edward Shortliffe, had been developing a large program called MYCIN – an expert system that knows about bacteraemia, that is bacteria in the blood, and meningitis, bacterial infection of the cerebro-spinal fluid. Purely as a test of its abilities, MYCIN was given the task of diagnosing patient 219 and suggesting a method of treatment for her.

MYCIN operates as a consultant, asking questions about the patient and the results of her tests and building up from the answers a decision about the likeliest causes of her illness. After just fourteen questions it had correctly identified meningitis; after forty-one it had narrowed it down to tuberculous meningitis and the consultation was completed after forty-six questions with a recommendation of treatment.

Part of patient 219's consultation is shown overleaf; it demonstrates well how MYCIN handles problems and moves decisively forward to its diagnosis and prescription.

Patient 219's consultation

Please enter information about the patient.
1) Name   Age   Sex   Race
★★ Pt219   42 YEARS   FEMALE   LATINO
2) Are there any positive cultures obtained from Pt219?
★★ NO
3) Are there any pending cultures of Pt219?
★★ YES
4) Site   Date collected   Stain examined?   Method of collection
★★ CSF   3-JUN-75   YES   N/A

[MYCIN goes on to ask various other questions]

13) Has Pt219 recently had symptoms of persistent headache or other abnormal neurologic symptoms (dizziness, lethargy, etc.)?
★★ YES
14) Has Pt219 recently had objective evidence of abnormal neurologic signs (nuchal rigidity, comas, seizures, etc.) documented by physician, observation or examination?
★★ YES

The CSF cultures will be considered to be associated with MENINGITIS.

[MYCIN has decided that meningitis is the most likely diagnosis and now starts to look for the particular infection that may be causing it. If the doctor who is using MYCIN is puzzled by any of the program's questions, typing 'WHY' makes MYCIN explain its reasoning in asking that question.]

20) For how many days has Pt219 had abnormal neurologic signs?
★★ UNKNOWN
21) For how many days has Pt219 had neurologic symptoms?
★★ 9 DAYS
22) Has Pt219 had recent evidence of tender or enlarged salivary glands?
★★ WHY
<3.0> This will aid in determining the type of the infection. It has already been established that <3.1> the infection which requires therapy is meningitis. Therefore, if <3.2> Pt219 has shown symptoms of mumps then there is weakly suggestive evidence (.4) that the type of the infection is viral. (Author: Yu).
★★ NO
23) Has Pt219 been exposed to any contagious disease recently (e.g. menigococcal disease, mumps)?
★★ NO

[The ability of MYCIN (and most other expert systems) to explain what they are doing is quite vital. Not only does it give the user a check on what the computer is up to, but it may also have an educational value, just like working with an experienced consultant will develop the knowledge and experience of a junior doctor. Notice that after explaining why it had asked question 22, MYCIN quoted the name of the doctor who had written that rule into the program so that it could be checked back further. As MYCIN proceeds with its consultation it reaches an area that is outside its knowledge, so it asks the doctor for an opinion and then checks if it is safe for it to continue.]

39) Is Pt219's chest X-ray suggestive of ACTIVE-TB?
★★ YES

40) (What is the infection which you feel would account for any organism isolated from the pending sputum culture (CULTURE-2)?
★★ PNEUMONITIS

The SPUTUM cultures will be considered to be associated with PNEUMONIA.

41) Please give the date on which clinical evidence (symptoms, signs or laboratory tests) of the pneumonia first appeared.
★★ 25-May-75

NOTE: the MYCIN system currently has rules for dealing with the following infection: BACTEREMIA MENINGITIS. Because its rule set is still incomplete, all other infections will be treated like bacteremia. Consequently MYCIN may not be able to correctly determine the identity or significance of the organisms causing this pneumonia, or to recommend appropriate therapy.
Would you like to continue the consultation anyway?
★★ YES

I have found evidence (RULE 523 RULE 579) that treatment should cover for Mycobacterium-tb causing meningitis.
I have found evidence (RULE 565) that treatment should cover for Coccidoides causing meningitis.
I have found evidence (RULE 565 RULE 570) that treatment should cover for Cryptococcus causing meningitis.

[MYCIN has correctly diagnosed the disease and it now moves into its second phase – deciding on the treatment most suitable for this particular patient.]

44) Is Pt219 pregnant or breast feeding?
★★ NO
45) Do you have reason to suspect that Pt219 may have impaired renal function?
★★ NO
46) Pt219's weight in kilograms
★★ 51.3

My preferred therapy recommendation is as follows:
Give the following in combination:

1) ETHAMBUTAL
Dose: 1.28g (13.0 100mg-tablets) q24h PO for 60 days (calculated on basis of 25 mg/kg) then 770 mg (7.5 100mg-tablets) q24h PO (calculated on basis of 15 mg/kg).
(The dose should be modified in renal failure. I can adjust the dose only if a creatinine clearance or a serum creatinine is obtained.)
Comments: Periodic vision screening tests are recommended for optic neuritis.

2) INH
Dose: 513mg (5.0 100mg-tablets) q24h PO (calculated on basis of 10 mg/kg).

3) RIFAMPIN
Dose: 600mg PO q24h
Comments: Adminster dose on an empty stomach.

Although I suspect that fungus may be a possible pathogen, in the absence of definitive evidence, I will not recommend antifungal therapy at this time.

MYCIN had performed perfectly. Not only did it reach the correct conclusions, but it indicated its areas of uncertainty, asked the human doctor's advice about a point that was outside its expertise, explained its decisions and suggested additional treatment to cover other possible infections which might be involved. These abilities, which MYCIN first established, are crucially important if expert systems are to be of use in the real world where answers may be unknown or uncertain and where the people who will rely on these programs need to be given a window onto the internal workings of the electronic expert.

MYCIN was one of a group of three expert systems produced in the early 1970s at Stanford University in California. They were distinguished trendsetters – the first truly knowledge-based programs ever written. One of them, called DENDRAL, is now a world authority on the technique of chemical analysis known as spectroscopy. This is an absolute cornerstone of modern science, with applications that range from astronomy to pharmacology. But it requires great skill to interpret its results, which come in the form of a very long list of numbers or an extremely complex graph. Yet, within this field, DENDRAL's reputation is so high that scientists are prepared to risk their professional status by publishing results on the strength of DENDRAL's judgment, without reference to any human authority.

The third program of the trio is called PROSPECTOR and its task is to assess geological data in order to guide mining companies towards new deposits. It has not yet had very much unsupervised use, but it did recently discover, by itself, a worthwhile and unexpected deposit of molybdenum on Mount Tolman in the northwestern United States. Subsequent drilling tests have confirmed that the region most favoured by PROSPECTOR does indeed contain high-grade ore.

Living by the rules

At the heart of all these expert systems lie simple rules. These are not algorithms defining a sequence of operations but knowledge rules designed to produce conclusions from already known facts. For example, a couple of typical rules in a car maintenance system might be:

1. IF the engine will not start
   AND there is fuel in the tank
   THEN check the battery.
2. IF Rule 1 has been used
   AND the battery is all right
   THEN check the distributor

Such rules are the system's store of knowledge: they are the expertise that allows it to draw sensible conclusions from simple items of information such as 'the engine does not start', 'there is plenty of fuel in the tank' and so on. When it is being used, the system contains both knowledge and information – knowledge about cars in general and information about this particular car. As the store of information builds

This copper mine in Montana is so vast that it dwarfs the town on its rim. Picking the right spot to dig such a hole is a major gamble — in future, expert systems may take the decision

Field geologists must carry a great deal of expertise around in their heads. Computers are unlikely to replace that skill but they could make the job simpler and more reliable

up it brings into play different rules, prompting further requests for information and working towards a sensible diagnosis of the problem.

An expert was once defined as 'one who knows more and more about less and less', and this is certainly a characteristic of all expert systems. They operate within narrow and highly specialized areas of knowledge: there is no expert system in common sense, nor is there ever likely to be one (which is not to say that there can never be a computer program with common sense, simply that it is not going to be an expert system). But, given that constraint, the range of applications of expert systems is virtually limitless.

One extremely successful expert system is used by a major manufacturer of large computers. Starting from the customer's order it produces a complete list of all the main units, sub-assemblies and small parts that are needed in order to put together the required customized system. It works out everything down to the plugs, cables and other trivia and then produces a floor plan of the whole layout.

In a totally different sphere is an expert system developed for one of the big international oil companies. Its knowledge domain is political risk analysis. If the company is considering building a refinery or a chemical plant in a Third World country the investment, and therefore the risk, can be colossal. The role of the expert system is to assess that country's political, social and economic stability and advise on the likelihood of nationalization, civil disturbance, appropriation of assets and other such threats. The human experts who can make such judgments are rare and widely scattered. A computerized expert would be able to give managers rapid access to advice.

From there it is easy to see that the field is wide open. If political, economic and medical rules can be given to an expert system then why not legal, ethical, psychiatric or religious ones? Is there any rational reason (there may well be emotional ones) why we should not accept marriage guidance counselling, psychiatric therapy or a prison sentence from a computer that has absorbed the wisdom of many human authorities in the subject? The moral implications in such types of expert system obviously deserve our careful attention, but it ought to be said now that all the existing expert systems seem to have been used with great ethical caution.

Certainly, no one's life has yet been entrusted to an expert system's judgment – although it may not be long before our deaths might be. An example of how an expert system may help in a very difficult and sensitive area is a program that advises on the care of terminally ill cancer patients. It is being developed by the Imperial Cancer Research Fund in conjunction with a hospice that provides care for the dying.

The aim of this system is, quite simply, to make the patient's final weeks more pleasant. Cancer is not a single disease but a large and very diverse group of them, and the range of symptoms that they produce is every bit as varied. Even when the symptoms appear quite familiar, the

An oil refinery in the tropics is a major investment – the risks it faces have as much to do with politics as with engineering

fact that terminal patients will not be troubled by long-term side effects allows the use of drugs that are not normally prescribed. This, taken together with the effects some anti-cancer therapies may produce, results in a subject where considerable skill and experience can be required to prescribe the best treatment. Junior doctors or GPs cannot be expected to have such specialist skills, yet may be called upon to help. The hope is that this expert system, when complete, will offer them ready access to this valuable knowledge.

But what are the implications of putting our trust in a computer program? How far should we allow it to tell us what to do? One obvious area of difficulty is to do with responsibility, particularly where people's well-being is directly concerned. If a patient is treated solely according to the recommendations of a computer program who should be held responsible if anything goes wrong? Should it be the doctor who referred the patient to the expert system? Should it be the specialists whose expertise is contained within it, or should it be the computer programmer who made it work?

The decision, taken early on by the creators of MYCIN, that expert systems should be able to explain their reasoning at every step, has been followed by most other workers in this field. Many believe that we should be trying to produce programs that can be argued and debated with just as any human expert can. But for this to happen we shall need some powerful new techniques that allow the expert system to look at the way in which it is making use of its knowledge. At rock bottom all of us rely on simple facts and ideas that we take for granted and could not explain any further; the same is true of any expert system. We give it knowledge about its subject, but the way in which it uses that knowledge is programmed in as instructions; the computer does not 'know' how to do it, it simply does it. If we could put that part of the program that makes decisions at each step also into the knowledge base, then we would have a computer which could explain more about what it is doing. A few expert systems are being developed along these lines, but it is an ambitious task and one that we probably do not yet understand well enough.

Certainly, it will be very demanding in terms of computer power, and others have argued that in many cases we do not need such intellectual ability in a program anyway. After all most of us are prepared to entrust our lives to an aircraft that is being landed entirely by computers; why, then, should we not trust a knowledge-based computer in the same way? Of course there is a difference because, provided that the system does not fail physically, the computers used in an instrument landing system should give a safe touchdown every time, whereas a complex expert system like MYCIN can only achieve about 80 per cent agreement with human consultants. On the other hand, they often disagree with each other, too.

It is, in fact, surprisingly difficult to discover exactly what human experts know and how they use their knowledge. Uncovering this skill and transferring it into an expert system is a specialist task which has given rise to a whole new activity called knowledge engineering. The knowledge engineer may spend months or even years questioning and observing the human experts in order to understand how they reach decisions. As the expert system grows, the knowledge engineer modifies its rules so as to improve its performance. It is a slow process and one that the human experts can do little to help with. Years of experience do not lead to a carefully structured set of rules in the expert's head but rather a fuzzy mental mass of – well, expertise. Rather like walking a tightrope, expertise is something that becomes second nature; you cannot perform if you stop to think about every step.

One surprising outcome of this process is that, often, the rules contained in an expert system mean very little to the human experts whose knowledge it contains. It is not always clear whether this is because the human experts are not aware that this is how they think, or whether the computer has actually devised alternative rules that lead to the same

LEFT On-board computers can land an airliner virtually unaided – but would you trust your life as readily to a computerised doctor?

RIGHT Dealing on a commodity exchange calls for split-second shrewdness – it is no place for a conventional expert system

conclusions. Certainly it suggests that we need not try to re-create the ways in which people believe they think so long as the results are right.

The machines of the fifth generation will depend for their very foundations on the ability to handle knowledge, so it is important that we should think carefully about the ways in which knowledge is acquired and used. But it is important to realize that there is no one approach which is always appropriate. Human expertise comes in many different forms and computer expertise will have to do the same.

All the examples we have seen so far are of a type called consultative expert systems: we go to them for advice, they ask us questions and eventually they offer a recommendation. The whole process happens at a relatively relaxed pace; in some cases a large expert system may need to take 20 or even 30 seconds between questions. This is quite acceptable for some tasks, but there are many jobs that call for experts who can think on their feet and they demand a completely different type of expert system.

Blackboard jungle

In the City of London, away from the panelled rooms where port and cigars set a mellow pace to financial dealings, large fortunes are riding on a tide of adrenalin. The job of the commodity dealers must be one of the most stressful there is. Not only must they make the right decision about buying or selling, they must do it instantly – ten seconds delay could lose tens of thousands of pounds. Already it is a highly technological activity, making great use of computers and communications satellites, but recently expert system designers have started to look at ways of speeding up the process even further.

This is obviously no environment for a thoughtful consultative program. What is needed is an expert system which can continuously monitor the prevailing situation and so be able to offer instant advice at any moment. It should also be able to recognize likely movements in the market before they happen and, of course, to assess what effects its own decisions will have on other dealers. Programs like these are sometimes called blackboard systems because they achieve their speed by noting down current information in an area of computer memory, the blackboard; this is accessible by several different systems, which can assess it and compare their judgments of how to respond.

Another area where blackboard systems are being considered is in the interpretation of radar data for air traffic control. Like commodity trading, this requires complex decisions to be taken very rapidly; although in this case it is lives and not just money that may be lost. Work is already under way on developing an expert system that could help by providing constant interpretation of the radar picture in front of the air traffic controller. There is a vast amount of information involved in this: not just the present course of the plane, but also its flying characteristics, the weather conditions and the flight plan. A jumbo jet, for example, is less maneuverable than a smaller plane but also less affected by the weather; on the other hand, because of its size, it leaves a much longer wake of dangerously turbulent air behind it. Such factors all need to be taken into account when controlling aircraft within a restricted corridor, and having a blackboard system to keep an eye on these things could well help to make the whole process even safer.

Other applications of these systems will lie in power stations, military operations, the control of large assembly lines and similar areas where expert judgment needs to be called on at very short notice. In many of these cases time-consuming question-and-answer sessions are not only impossible but are not really needed because much of the information is already being handled by computer. The difficulty so far has been in finding how to represent knowledge in such a way that it can be used to process the data continuously. Ordinary consultative systems start with a clean slate and build up a store of information and a list of relevant rules until a logically watertight conclusion can be reached. Blackboard systems cannot do this because all the time new information is being added, old information is becoming irrelevant and different rules need to be applied. A good deal of research will be needed before we have an efficient way of coping with this.

Making up your own rules

The distinction between knowledge and information applies to all expert systems, consultative or blackboard. Knowledge is the store of rules about the subject in general; information consists of the details of this job in particular. Every time the expert system is used its store of information changes, but the rules are untouchable except by reference to the human experts who wrote them. This is reasonable enough but there are, surely, some circumstances in which the program could

Air traffic control already relies very heavily on computers but it is hoped that expert systems may ease some of the controllers' nerve racking responsibilities

adjust imperfect rules in the light of experience, or even create new ones if the evidence supports them.

This really is a thorny problem because experience may be a very bad guide. We all know from past experience that the sun will rise again tomorrow morning, but unless we have a broader knowledge of why it does so, we would be totally confused by a visit to the North Pole where it rises and sets only once a year. In the same way the car maintenance expert system might decide, on the strength of a run of faulty distributors, that they were the inevitable cause of electrical trouble and then get confused when presented with a weak battery.

Learning by experience is what philosophers call induction and it has led to some rather heated debate over the years. The problem is not that induction is useless – we use it pretty successfully most of the time – but rather that we do not have any means of telling when it is safe to use it and when it is not.

Having said that, it must be admitted that for a computer to have the ability to learn from experience (including the experience of getting it wrong) could be extremely useful. So, what are the prospects? A fair bit of research has been done and a number of approaches tried out. One type of program, developed at the University of Edinburgh, provides a rule-induction system allowing computers to produce the rules for a consultative expert system purely out of a series of examples. So there is no need for either the expert or a knowledge engineer to work out rules and put them into the computer. It will examine all the examples it has been given and extract the pattern they appear to fit. This pattern is unlikely, of course, to be perfect, but every time that it encounters a new example it can adjust its rules so as to give a closer fit to reality.

The two print-outs reproduced here show how this worked in producing a very simple expert system which advises on the maintenance of helicopter gearboxes. In deciding whether to remove a particular gearbox now or allow it a certain number of further flying hours, the mechanics looked at four possible symptoms: the type of debris in the gearbox casing, the weight of the debris, the level of vibration and the purity of the oil. On the basis of this information they could reach an instant decision and yet they did so on the basis of expertise, not by following rigid guidelines. When the eight examples were fed into the rule-induction program it was able, within a couple of minutes, to produce the set of rules shown in the second frame.

These rules form the basis of a consultative expert system, but they can also be of great value in themselves. For example, they show that vibration is the overriding factor which must be considered first; even if the expert system is never used as such, this one fact could be of great use in speeding up routine maintenance checks or for training future mechanics. In fact rule induction may prove to have a very wide range of uses quite outside the field of expert systems. Wherever people take decisions in an informal or intuitive way they build up a complex network of judgments without being able to say why they do it in that particular way. The ability to pry out the underlying beliefs can be a very valuable tool.

BELOW LEFT Rule induction. These eight examples come from actual helicopter gearboxes. For each one the computer is told the type and weight of debris in the gearbox, the level of vibration, the oil purity and what decision had been taken about the number of hours which that gearbox would be allowed to continue flying

BELOW RIGHT Using the eight examples, the computer has produced these rules for use in an expert system. If the vibration is high the gearbox must be removed regardless of any other factor. If it is medium and the oiltaint is less than 23 then look at the type and weight of debris. If vibration is low and oiltaint is less than 17 then look at the debris type. These rules may not be perfect yet but they took only a few minutes to produce compared to days of work with conventional methods

```
EXPERT-EASE   file: GEARBOX    28304 bytes left         1 : Debristyp
          logical   integer   logical    integer
          Debristyp Debriswt  Vibration  Oiltaint   Remove
1         coarse    20        *          *          remove
2         fine      3         low        3          hrs50
3         fine      3         medium     3          hrs25
4         *         *         high       *          remove
5         *         *         *          30         remove
6         fine      3         medium     15         hrs5
7         coarse    1         medium     3          hrs5
8         coarse    2         medium     3          remove

editing examples
↑,↓,←,→, !, new, delete, move, change, xpand, help ? ('+' for more)
)
```

```
EXPERT-EASE   file: GEARBOX    28368 bytes left              1
Vibration
   high : remove
   medium : Oiltaint
              <23 : Debristyp
                     coarse : Debriswt
                              <2 : hrs5
                              >=2 : remove
                     fine : Oiltaint
                              <9 : hrs25
                              >=9 : hrs5
              >=23 : remove
   low : Oiltaint
              <17 : Debristyp
                     coarse : remove
                     fine : hrs50
              >=17 : remove

viewing rule
↑,↓, attributes, files, examples, new, run, print ?
```

A property developer who bought houses for improvement and resale believed that one of the factors that affected his decision whether or not to buy was the area of town where the house was situated. When a record of his past decisions was fed into the rule-induction program it found that the price and nature of the property were dominant, but that location had played no part at all in his choices. This is a minor example but on a larger scale, the ability to root out mistaken beliefs could have a significant effect in making any organization more efficient.

As a management tool, programs that can extract patterns from a set of events offer not only the prospect of improving your own efficiency, but also of examining what lies behind your competitors' activities. Rule induction, for example, provides quite an effective way of studying the pricing policy behind a range of products. You just enter the prices and specifications of, say, all available food mixers and ask the system to extract the pattern they fit in with. You might find, for example, that it is the capacity of the bowl that tends to set the price level, that a juice extractor is worth an extra $20, but that the number of basic mixing attachments has little effect.

This is a far cry from mineral prospecting, caring for the dying or guiding aircraft, but it helps to demonstrate how versatile the ability to handle knowledge can be. As knowledge-based systems develop, and they are still in their infancy, we can expect computers to be applied to a wider range of problems than anyone predicts even now. Whoever is prepared for that expansion will be in a strong position to profit from it. Certainly the significance of knowledge processing has not been lost on the creators of Japan's Fifth Generation Computer Project. Their economic planners point to the fact that Japan has almost no natural resources of her own, so large-scale manufacturing industries will gradually become less profitable. The key to the future is seen to be in the service industries, which can create value with very little consumption of raw materials or energy. To this end Japan intends to establish a 'knowledge industry' in which computers act as 'amplifiers of knowledge', transforming and improving upon the brainpower of 'knowledge workers'. The stepping stones to this ambition are:

    1985: completion of the Functional Device Project for new chips
    1989: completion of the National Super Speed Computer Project
    1992: completion of the Fifth Generation Computer Project

This is the cold wind that has blown through the computer halls of Europe and the United States, and it is why so much commercial as well as academic muscle is being put into developing knowledge-based computers. Whatever may be said at international conferences about cooperation, this is a race that the competitors are treating as deadly serious. As one American computer scientist noted after a visit to Japan's Fifth Generation planners: 'They were very smart, very well prepared and they kept their mouths shut.'

CHAPTER THREE
Modern Architecture

Before the fifth generation came four others.

The first was the generation of clanking, glowing machines which filled vast rooms. The electromechanical Harvard Mark 1 belongs here as do ENIAC, LEO, MADM and other machines of the early '50s with their thousands of glowing vacuum tubes. But even while the first generation was getting started, its downfall was already taking shape. In July 1948 a short letter was published in The Physical Review Journal: it announced the invention by the Americans John Bardeen, Walter Houser Brattain and William Bradford Shockley of the transistor.

The second generation, the generation of transistorized computers, flickered briefly into life with a small machine produced in England at Manchester University in 1953, but did not really become established until the late 1950s. Its achievement was to make computers smaller, cheaper and more reliable. It lasted until the mid-1960s and the development of the integrated circuit.

The coming of the chip took computers into the third generation, a time of faster, more powerful machines and of rapid miniaturization. For the first time it became possible to make small machines: minicomputers appeared, no bigger than a small piece of furniture, and soon after came microcomputers that could sit on a desk. This was the time when computers began to enter our everyday lives.

With no sharp dividing line the third generation is now merging into the fourth with the development of VLSI: very large-scale integration. This brings memory chips which can store over a million bits of information in a few square millimetres and microprocessors as powerful as a large computer of the third generation. Computers are commonplace.

The fourth generation will see us through to the end of the 1980s. After that comes the fifth generation and a new direction. The changes that have characterized the first four generations have all been changes in the basic electronic technology out of which computers are made. In that sense they were changes that occurred outside the realm of computing and have not been restricted to it. Many other fields such as hi-fi and telecommunications have been dramatically altered by this progression of technologies and have helped to drive it forward.

The changes that will bring into being the fifth generation are entirely different. They are changes that arise out of the innermost depths of the computer, changes in the way in which its internal operations are organized. Of course, they will demand continued progress in electronics, but it is not that progress in itself that will bring about the next generation.

The new machines – the knowledgeable personal assistants, the intelligent computers – will require to be built on different lines. The coming generation gap is not like that between valves and transistors, but rather more like the gulf between calculators and computers. It is a change of architecture.

Fourth generation chip. Looking more like an intricate tapestry than a computer circuit, this VLSI memory chip, seen here under the microscope, can store 288,000 bits of information

Designing time and space

When John von Neumann wrote the First Draft he set the computer free from some of the limitations of time. Because of its stored program, a von Neumann machine is no longer bound by the speed and order of its incoming instructions, nor by the rate at which it can print out its results. It now made sense to build faster machines, machines so fast that no paper tape reader or typing finger could ever keep up. As computing speeds became even faster, time sharing was invented so that many people could use the machine simultaneously, each apparently getting the computer's undivided attention as it leaped and danced between them. Von Neumann released the computer to do what it does best – process patterns of pulses very, very fast.

But there was a price to pay. The freedom to make better use of time meant a restriction in the use of space. A layout, or architecture as computer people call it, was imposed on the computer. The various operational parts of the machine had to be connected together in a particular arrangement, and the data it handled had to move along certain well-defined paths. These factors which, more than anything else, allowed the computer to become a truly general-purpose machine are now starting to be a liability. The von Neumann design is being referred to as the von Neumann bottleneck.

The architecture von Neumann created consists of two main regions connected by a highway. At one end of it is the central processing unit, or CPU, which follows the instructions contained in the program and does all the actual work of manipulating the data. At the other end is the memory, which stores everything that the CPU will need: the programs which tell it what to do, the raw data which it must handle, and any temporary jottings and partially worked out results which it needs to note down. The highway connecting these two regions and carrying data in both directions between them is called the data bus.

The CPU works as both master and slave. It contains the control unit, an all-seeing taskmaster who ensures that everything is done in the correct order, that no data is lost and no processes clash. Nothing moves on the data bus except under the control unit's command, no calculation proceeds except on its authority. Work stops and starts as it dictates so as to keep everything in step.

The slave who actually does much of the work is called the Arithmetic and Logic Unit – the ALU. This is a cluster of gates and other circuits that can manipulate patterns of pulses according to various simple rules. As we saw in Chapter One, the pulses in a computer are arranged into words of 8, 16, 32 or even more individual binary bits: 1s and 0s. The sort of thing the ALU can do is to take two such words and add them together or to change a particular bit within a word. Out of such simple activities all the achievements of a computer are built up.

At the other end of the data bus sits the memory. This is arranged rather like a vast warehouse of small pigeon holes, each one of which

MADM – the Manchester Automatic Digital Machine was the world's first computer to make use of a stored program. Developed at the University of Manchester, it ran its first program on 21 June 1948

has its own identification number, or address as it is called. Within the pigeon holes are stored the pulse words. To gain access to any part of its stored information the CPU merely has to send the memory an address number and a signal saying, 'I want to read the contents of this address', and the pulse pattern that is stored there will travel up the data bus. To store a number it specifies an address and 'writes' the number into that memory location. How does it know which addresses to use? They themselves may be stored as numbers in other addresses, or may be the result of a calculation. Ultimately it is the programs we put in that determine all of it.

It is a wonderfully flexible system. By centralizing all of the computation in one place and all of the storage in another, the von Neumann architecture provided equally fast access to any part of any program or any item of data that was stored inside it, as well as the ability to modify programs as easily as if they were data. The difficulty is the highway. To be sure it is a very high-speed, multi-lane (one for each bit so that a whole word travels in unison) highway; but it can only take a single word at a time. So, in spite of the massive improvement in speed, and even though the program instructions no longer need to be followed in a strictly predetermined order, the computer is still operating sequentially: one step after another, each one completed before the next can begin. This is the von Neumann bottleneck.

What is needed is a new architecture: a building style that will eliminate the bottleneck and thereby reduce the time being wasted by the processor as it waits for data and instructions to funnel in and out at every step. Like all new styles it needs a name and this one is called 'parallel architecture'. 'Parallel' because it will allow several operations to take place at the same time, in parallel, rather than forcing them to follow each other sequentially.

Everyone is agreed that the parallel approach is the way to make computers more efficient, but there is rather less consensus about just how it should be done. Different designs with names like pipeline, systolic, NON-VON, reduction, and dataflow offer various solutions to the problem of making computers significantly faster. Which will prove to be the most useful remains to be seen, but it is essential that some effective new architecture is created if the fifth generation plans are to work. The timetable for success is, once again, set by Japan which has said that its National Superspeed Computer Project will make a machine one thousand times faster than today's fastest computer by 1989.

Parallel architecture
One of the simpler techniques, which is used on several of today's supercomputers, is pipelining. It is a very appropriate name. Consider a relatively simple task like multiplying two numbers together; this is far too difficult for the ALU to manage in one go and can only be achieved if it is broken down into many simple steps. Every time we ask it to multiply, this sequence of instructions will be found in the memory and carried out one by one. If we need to do a thousand different multiplications, it will be run through a thousand times.

At each stage of the process, another instruction and perhaps some data will need to be sent between the memory and the CPU. Suppose, however, that we assembled a chain of simple processing units each of which is set up to do one step in the total sequence and then pass its outcome on to the next unit. Two numbers fed into the start of this pipeline will eventually emerge from the other end as the answer we seek. At every step the partially worked-out solution moves on to the next section of pipe and we can put in another pair of numbers behind it. Once the pipeline is full, completed answers pour out of the end as fast as new numbers go in at the front.

If the pipeline contains, say, thirty steps then in effect it is working simultaneously on thirty different multiplications. To do just a few calculations in this way is pretty inefficient, but think of the weather forecasting computer working its way through one third of a million points across the northern hemisphere, each one requiring exactly the same set of calculations to be applied to its particular data, then having to repeat the whole lot a hundred and twenty times. For tasks like that pipelining was a godsend.

If pipelining is rather like an assembly line then the other technique now being applied to some computers is more like building a prefabricated house. One workshop may be producing wall panels while another makes up window frames and a third prepares roof trusses. If the plans have been well prepared then the separate workshops can proceed completely independently without even having to know who else is involved or what they are doing. It is only at the final assembly stage that the products of their work need to come together. In the same

Fastest computer of the present generation. The Cray X-MP relies on pipeline architecture and its unusual shape to provide high computing speeds. The cylindrical layout has been chosen so as to keep to a minimum the distance that pulses need to travel

way, some computers are being developed with several independent processors each of which has its own memory and tackles a separate part of the overall program. Sooner or later their efforts have to be combined, but by distributing the work as far as possible we can achieve a significant increase in computing speed.

Typically, the machines currently being developed have between four and sixteen processors with a system for routeing data between each of them. But some computer designers are thinking really big. The NON-VON (non-von Neumann) project at Columbia University is beginning with a modest 256,000 processors, but is expected to expand to over a million individual processors by the end of the 1980s.

This machine's structure is different from other multi-processor computers in being arranged rather like a branching tree with one processor connected to two others, each of which connects to two more and so on. This sort of 'massively parallel' architecture is not going to be the answer to everyone's problems but for some applications, such as certain types of commercial data processing, it may well be a winner. The biggest difficulty it will have to overcome is likely to be reliability: if one of the processors high up in the chain breaks down it could put thousands of others out of action. This, as we shall see later, is in direct contrast to some parallel systems which will work perfectly, although rather more slowly, even if several of their processors are damaged.

Both pipelining and multiple-processor systems are already being used in commercial computers. Pipelining in particular is available on all present-day supercomputers and, given the right type of problem, can be very effective. Multi-processor computers are still rather rare: one of the first of these to go into regular use was a four-processor machine at the same ballistics testing ground where ENIAC was conceived forty years ago.

Pipelining and multi-processor arrays are each best suited to one type of problem and each demands rather special programming methods.

Given those two requirements, they are both very powerful new techniques for making computers more efficient. But not everyone believes that they are the final solution. According to some critics both also suffer from a familiar problem: well disguised, but unmistakably there, lurks the von Neumann bottleneck.

Distributed control

The problem is that, no matter how distributed and parallel the actual processing has become, the computer still needs central control to allocate the work, deal with those sections that cannot be tackled in parallel, and pull together the final outcome of the computation. The need to synchronize and monitor all these activities brings us back almost to where we started; the problem has been made much smaller but it has not been totally eliminated.

Some computer designers now believe that the only way to open out the bottleneck once and for all will be to distribute not only the processing tasks but also the control functions throughout the machine. No longer would a central 'foreman' supervise, synchronize and allocate the work; instead the work would, well, sort itself out.

It is an appealing idea – a computer that can do many things at once and organize itself so well that, once the computation has been set in motion, it will not require constant internal monitoring to keep things moving along smoothly. It is not, however, immediately obvious how best to achieve this. But what is clear is that the architecture of such a machine really would be very different. Not only would it do away with the central processing unit but the central memory would have to go as well. Imagine the confusion if many separate processors were all trying to fetch data and store data with no way of knowing whether another processor had already completed its part of the work, or perhaps had

LEFT Part of a highly parallel computer with 256 processors. It is used as a simulator of other computers so that new designs can be fully tested before they are built

RIGHT The Manchester University Dataflow computer with its designer Dr John Gurd. This design is likely to form the basis of the fifth generation machines which will be produced in the 1990s

even moved the required data to somewhere else. It would be total electronic anarchy.

Obviously supervision is still needed even if it no longer comes from one powerful central controller. But how can it be spread around and still work efficiently? Several schemes have been proposed. Of these one of the furthest advanced and most promising is a technique called dataflow, which is being developed at the University of Manchester and at several laboratories in other countries.

A number of separate processors are used and there is also a strong element of pipelining, but gone are the central memory and the controller checking every stage of the work. Instead the problem being tackled is broken down into steps such as 'Add these two numbers together', or 'Compare these two pulse words to see if they are the same'. Each of these steps requires an instruction to say what must be done and the data on which to do it. In a conventional von Neumann machine the instructions would be fetched from memory in the correct sequence, the data would then be fetched from memory, the instruction carried out and finally the answer would be put back into memory. In a dataflow computer the data and the relevant instruction travel together through the system as a self-contained package. Making sure that the right items of data come together and are combined with the correct instruction is done on the move by a process called 'token matching'.

Suppose that in a lengthy and complicated program we need to add two numbers together and then multiply this result with the outcome of another calculation which will be reached much later on in the process. A von Neumann machine would do the addition and then put away the answer in a known place in memory until it was needed for the final multiplication. But the dataflow approach is rather different: items of data have attached to them an additional group of binary bits called a 'tag' which is used to identify them. The combination of data and tag is known as a 'token'. If two tokens have matching tags they are packaged together and sent into a queue of other matched tokens waiting to be processed. If the matching unit cannot find a token's partner it puts it into a store of unmatched tokens.

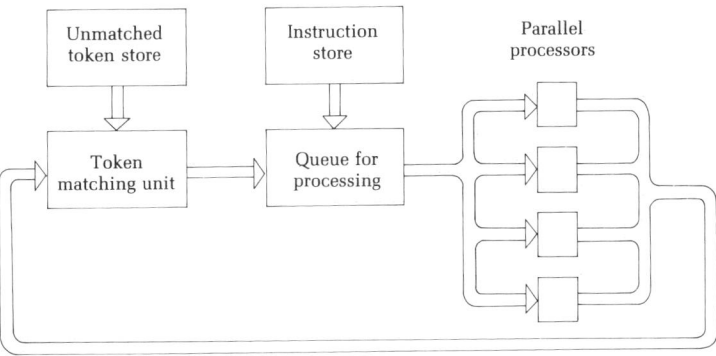

Architecture of the dataflow computer

Going back to the example, the two numbers to be added do have matching tags and so are sent to the next stage which checks the number of the tag and puts the appropriate instruction, 'Add', onto the package. Then they join the queue for the processing section until a processor becomes free to handle them.

When the result emerges it goes back around to the token matching unit. It cannot find a partner and so becomes an unmatched token until the number to be multiplied with it eventually appears. They go on to be processed and then come round again, perhaps to be matched with something else for further calculation.

With a system like this we never need to know which of several processors is doing what, nor worry too much about the sequence of processing since nothing inappropriate will be done to a token until all the necessary data are available. So long as the system can keep up enough flow to ensure that all the processors are kept fully occupied it ought to work very efficiently. The fact that there are several processing units and that some token packages are being processed while others are being matched, and yet others are having instructions attached, means that the dataflow computer is very much an example of parallel architecture. In the case of the University of Manchester dataflow machine there are twenty processing elements working simultaneously and another twenty tokens at a time going through the pipeline which matches them and prepares them for processing, giving forty parallel operations.

In principle there is no limit to how far the dataflow machine could be extended, although it does eventually run up against a speed restriction because of the time taken to check through the unmatched tokens at every step. It is, however, very reliable because matched tokens go to whichever processor becomes available. If any of them breaks down it will simply be ignored while the remaining ones handle the work. All that suffers is the speed of computation.

Research is still going on to refine the details of how a dataflow computer should best be designed and to work out all the new programming techniques it demands. But the first of the Manchester machines is now successfully running programs and it seems very likely that dataflow architecture will be used in Japan's fifth-generation machines.

Blueprint for a personal assistant
The emphasis on knowledge processing rather than just information processing, and on parallel architectures as opposed to the centralized von Neumann architecture, are two of the key elements in the current transformation of computing. But how do they relate to each other and to the aims of the fifth generation? How, in particular, do you set about designing a computer personal assistant with them?

The task is to produce a machine that can help us solve problems without demanding that we always tell it how to solve the problem.

This is a crucial point. Any computer can solve problems but in order for it to do so we must write or buy a program that contains the instructions for solving that problem. The fifth-generation machines will still need to have programs but these will be much more general: programs telling them how to write their own programs or where to find suitable programs in other computers. This will mean that most of us should never need to learn any programming languages nor become involved in the details of how they work.

This transformation from a tool to an assistant entails quite a major change of emphasis within the machine: it is no longer the part that follows the instructions contained in the program that is most important, but the part that issues these instructions. Master and slave are still contained within the same machine but magnified and reflected many times over in a hall of mirrors. The machine *is* a computer, but it also knows about computers; it obeys computer programs, but it also creates computer programs; it contains expert systems which include expert systems about the use of expert systems.

This is what the plan of a personal assistant looks like.

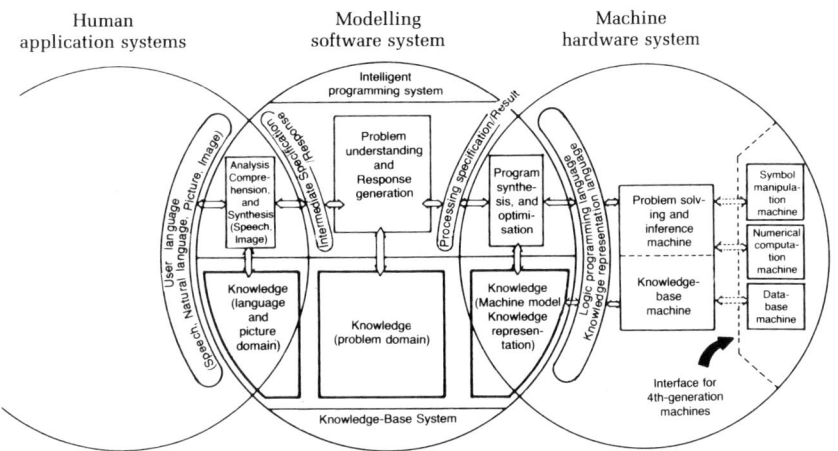

There are two things to notice straight away. Firstly, the three circles: the one on the left is the computer's link to you, the one on the right is its link to the more or less conventional computing equipment contained within it. The heart of the fifth-generation computer, the middle circle, separates the two so that the user never communicates directly with the part that does the donkey work. Secondly, there is a division that runs through the three circles; below the centre line the word 'knowledge' appears several times – these are the machine's knowledge bases, its expert systems. Knowledge processing is the foundation of this design, and parallel architecture is its framework.

On the left, the machine communicates with us through its user language. Most importantly, this is the ability to understand and use natural languages – English, Japanese, etc. But it is not restricted to entry at a keyboard: it can just as easily use speech and accept handwritten or printed papers which it scans optically. We can also show it pictures or diagrams and ask it to display its results as a chart or a drawing if we prefer.

This one part of the project is more than enough of a challenge. Not even the best of today's efforts can manipulate language, pictures or speech well enough for this sort of task. The next two chapters examine these topics in more detail, but it is worth noting now that this is an area where the amount of computing involved is so great that parallel processing will be absolutely essential. The box marked 'analysis, comprehension and synthesis' is where this happens. It rests firmly on its knowledge bases: expert systems for dealing with sentence structure, grammar, diagrammatic techniques, object recognition and so on. Once this stage has been passed, but before the computer actually starts to tackle the problem, it has a rough idea of what it is being told to do and can ask questions if anything is unclear.

The next step is the central one, the one that comes closest to intelligence: it is understanding the problem, which is not the same as understanding the words that expressed the problem. Suppose that somebody hands you a broken television set and asks you to repair it. It is easy to understand what you are being asked to do but, unless you happen to be a trained TV mechanic, you are unlikely to understand the problem of how actually to do it. This same distinction applies to the computer: first it must understand the words that tell it what the problem is, then it must understand the problem itself.

Here again the whole enterprise rests on a foundation of knowledge bases. Some of these will apply to the specific subject areas you and your computer work with, others will help the computer to find out what it does not know. For example, if you ask it to make an airline booking for you it does not need to have all the schedules within it, but simply to know which external computer to call up in order to check departure times and book the seat. Such transfer of knowledge and information between computers is, of course, already happening all the time but at the moment it requires direct instructions from us at every step. A fifth-generation computer will require only a single command: 'Book me on a flight to Paris on Tuesday morning', from which it will work out what to do, taking into account which airlines you prefer, how long it will take you to get from home to the airport, what other commitments you might have that day and so on.

Up to this stage the computer has worked out what you want it to do and checked its subject knowledge to see what factors need to be taken into account and what extra information and knowledge it requires. One more step remains before we can leave the middle circle – it must now convert this understanding of what is required into the step-by-step instructions that will make it happen. The centre of attention shifts now from the problem to the machine itself. What began as a general request to work out some sales figures, for example, became more detailed as the particular information was identified and the process of additions, averages and so on was assembled. But all this was abstract; now it has to be married up with the reality of how the computer can tackle it.

The right-hand side of the middle circle is in fact a computer program that writes computer programs. It uses the understanding which has now been achieved to create a set of instructions that will tell the machine's processors how to combine and manipulate the data in order to solve the problem. Program-writing programs do already exist, but they are not yet good enough to cope with all the tasks a fifth-generation computer will have to tackle. Again this is an area that will need to rely on knowledge: in this case self-knowledge, the computer's understanding of how it itself works and how it can be programmed.

Whenever we program a computer we make use of a programming language. This is a way of telling the machine what it has to do in a form which it can translate into simple operations on pulse patterns. Looking at it from another angle, the language is a way of representing the problem we wish to solve. When a computer writes computer programs it, too, needs to use a language and this is what the curved box marked 'logic programming language/knowledge representation language' is concerned with. Traditional computer languages like Basic, Fortran or Cobol are not at all well suited to handling knowledge or very general types of problem, so newer types of language are being devised for the fifth generation. One of these, called Prolog, is already available and quite widely used in developing the techniques that will be needed.

Beyond this point we are dealing with more or less conventional computing, albeit using very fast parallel architectures such a dataflow. The machine now has the necessary information, knowledge and logical understanding of the problem. All that is left is to perform the actual manipulation of the data and then pass the results back up through the various stages which will package and present it according to our needs. We will end up with print, speech, pictures or perhaps no apparent result, just an automatic telephone transfer of data or an increase in the computer's knowledge and experience.

At rock bottom this great edifice is built entirely on the familiar combination of processors and memory, together handling patterns of electrical pulses. To that extent computers will remain unchanged, but they will be built according to new architectures, will operate with new-found knowledge and will play a new role in people's lives. For those of us who are not much interested in the details of what goes on inside this will be the most obvious change: computers will become easy to use. We shall still tell them what to do but they will work out how to do it. The versatile tool will become the intelligent assistant.

Or will it?

CHAPTER FOUR
Thinkchips

Intelligence, like truth and beauty, eludes the grasp of definition. Of course, we all know what it is but any attempt to pin it down invariably shimmers into uncertainty when looked at too closely. What, then, do we mean when we speak of an intelligent computer? Do we really want an electronic brain? Is it possible? The debate about artificial intelligence is one of the most contentious in modern science and certainly one of the most important in the field of computing. It concerns not just our relationship to computers but also to ourselves. Intelligent machines threaten us with imitation – the most dangerous form of flattery – but they also tempt us with new awareness.

Although intelligent machinery has had a long history in myth and fiction, it only became a serious topic for consideration with the invention of the general-purpose machine. That event, which marked the conception of computing, occurred in Cambridge. A young Fellow of King's College, called Alan Turing, was responsible.

Computable numbers

By any standards, Alan Turing was a remarkable man: a profound mathematician who delighted in his teddy bear and in listening to stories for children; an accomplished athlete who was noted for being clumsy and uncoordinated. A complex and probably unhappy man, he was distinctly not like other people. Those who knew him have recalled, mostly with affection, his unconventionality: the gasmask he wore as a protection against pollen, the mug chained and padlocked to his office radiator, the bicycle whose chain always fell off after a certain number of revolutions – rather than repair it he counted the revolutions as he rode and leaped off at the correct moment to hook it back on.

But eccentricity was not all he had to offer. His work on cracking the German Enigma code provided Britain with one of its strongest weapons in the Second World War, prompting Jack Good, another mathematician working for British Intelligence, to write: 'I won't say that what Turing did made us win the war but I daresay we might have lost it without him.' Although a mathematician by training, with degrees from Cambridge and Princeton, Turing's interests were always wide-ranging: theoretical work he did on the development of embryos still continues to offer new insights into morphogenesis, the study of how living organisms grow into a particular form.

But it was through mathematics that Alan Turing came to make his contribution to computing. It was probably the most important step forward that has ever been made in the subject, and all the more remarkable because it was made before computers had been invented.

In 1936 Alan Turing wrote a paper entitled 'On Computable Numbers with an Application to the *Entscheidungsproblem*'. It was a complex work, impenetrable by any except other mathematicians, but even they did not realize at the time what prophecies it contained. The main purpose of Turing's paper was to deal with the final remaining problem

ABOVE Alan Turing, one of the most important and most enigmatic figures in the development of computing

OPPOSITE Robots can assemble a car body with great precision but they usually rely on each part being in exactly the right place. Robot vision would make them far more flexible but it is still a long way off

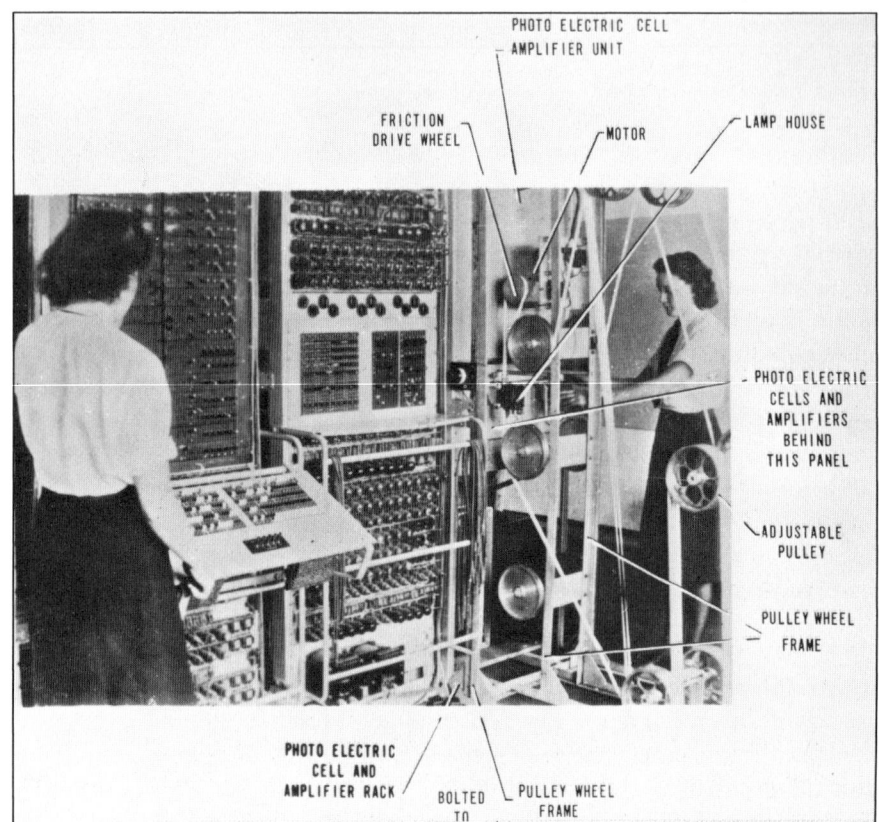

Colossus, the machine which Alan Turing helped to design in order to crack the German wartime Enigma code. It has often been described as the first electronic computer, in fact it was not a computer because it was not a general purpose machine but it did introduce many of the techniques on which electronic computers were later based

in a major mathematical conflict which had been going on since 1900. This concerned the question of whether all of mathematics was, at least in principle, provable, consistent and soluble.

To tackle this problem Turing imagined a simple machine consisting of an infinitely long paper tape divided along its length into squares, each square being either blank or containing a written symbol. This tape passes through a device which can read, write or erase the contents of whichever square is currently within it. Reading a symbol can change the 'state' of the device and so change the way in which it will respond to the next square it comes to. Using the idea of this extremely simple machine, Turing considered how it would cope with a tape on which the symbols represented those of mathematics and the changes of state were ones that obeyed the laws of mathematics. As the tape moved back and forth through the machine, a mathematical proof or calculation could be done. Given the correct sequence of symbols it should eventually be able to write onto the tape the required answer or conclusion.

Turing called his imaginary device a 'computer' (a word that until then had only been applied to people) and with its aid was able to prove that anything that can be done in mathematics can be done by such a machine in a finite number of steps. Some problems, however, would keep the machine busy for ever and so are permanently beyond mathematical solution. This result was of such importance that, at the time, it rather obscured Turing's other creation: he had invented the idea of the general-purpose machine. Since it can solve everything that is soluble the machine is now called a 'universal computer' or, more usually, a 'Turing machine'.

By 1936 mechanical calculators were well known but they were all highly specific pieces of hardware. What Turing did was to create the notion of software and show that new calculations did not need new bits of machinery but simply new instructions. Once the computer was built the rest was all programming. But at the time he thought of all this there were no computers and nobody had heard of programs. Undaunted by this minor complication Turing filled in the time until computers became available by paper computing – writing down the program instructions and following them through as if he were the machine (although he was too forgetful to be a very good computer).

The publication of 'On Computable Numbers' was the foundation of computing. More than that, Turing's discovery that everything which can be done with symbols can be done by a machine that manipulates symbols *is* computing. At the time, however, nobody had any idea if, or when, it would be possible to build such a machine. Certainly, Turing's computer of the imagination was never intended to be an engineering blueprint; its description was deliberately pared down to the barest essentials because it was necessary for Turing's purpose to show that everything the computer does can be contained in the instructions, without any need for clever mechanical tricks. But at least people could now be certain that, when they came, computers would not be a disappointment.

This would have been true even if computers were restricted to mathematics, but Turing's findings applied equally to any activity that could be specified in terms of symbols and rules: the use of language, musical composition, map reading, games of intellectual skill such as chess. And if a computer could be programmed with all these abilities then surely it would be programmed with intelligence.

That all depends on what you mean by intelligence

At one time intelligence lay somewhere between knowledge, cleverness and quick-wittedness. To be intelligent you needed a good education and a lively mind; it was a peculiarly human quality. Intelligence as we know it today is an invention of the twentieth century and, many would say, not a very useful one. In 1904 the French Ministry of Public Instruction wished to study the education of mentally retarded children in the schools of Paris and asked the psychologist Alfred Binet to prepare a series of tests which would measure mental ability. He devised a set of thirty problems intended to test reasoning and judgment rather than factual knowledge. Ten years later the US Army, faced with a massive intake because of the First World War, refined these tests in order to select potential officer material and to reject the retarded. These tests, largely based on patterns of shapes, numbers and letters, were the start of IQ (intelligence quotient) testing.

Alfred Binet, originator of the intelligence test

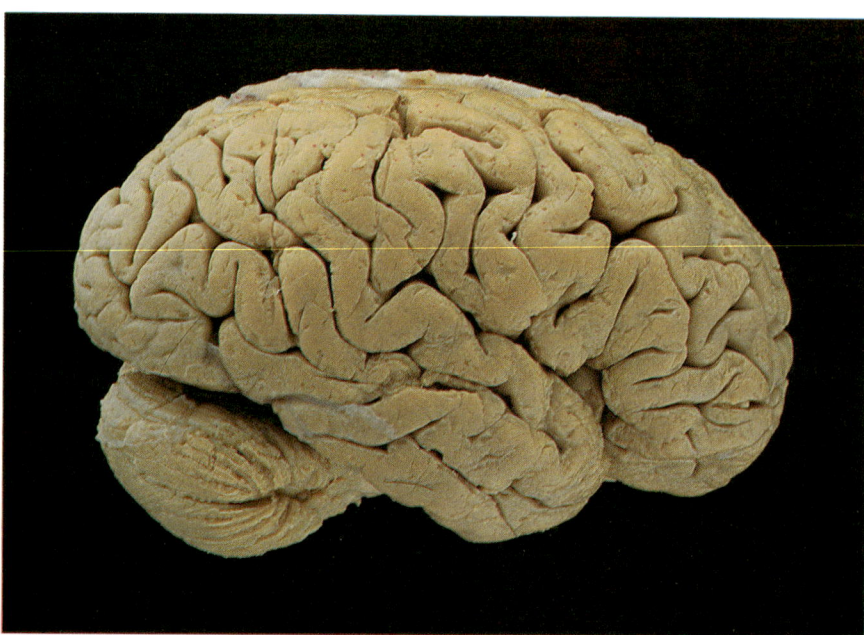

The human brain. Many scientists in the late 40s and early 50s believed that it would be possible to create a real thinking brain out of electronic circuits

Brain cells, shown here magnified 20 times. Electronic gates can imitate some of their characteristics but their behavior is much more complex than was once believed

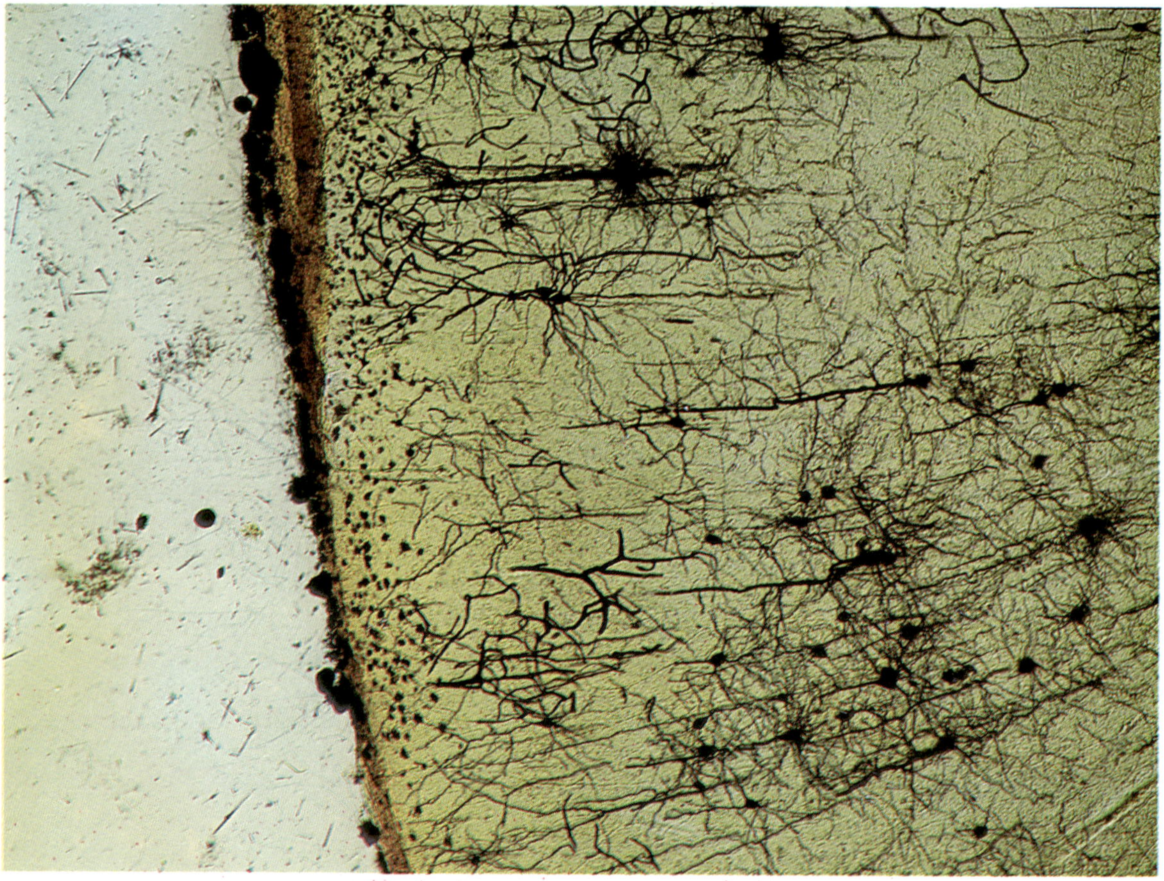

By these means intelligence became linked to logical and semi-mathematical abilities. You may never have learned much at school but if you were intelligent, so the argument went, you would instantly be able to sort, rearrange, manipulate and draw conclusions from the abstract symbols in front of you. Playing chess, proving geometrical theorems, solving mathematical problems – these were the sorts of activities that exemplified intelligence. And the Turing machine could do them all.

Turing himself seems to have had little doubt that an intelligent computer was perfectly feasible. From the very start his work with the paper computer which he had devised was directed not at serious scientific calculation but at the development of a chess-playing program. A few years later, just as the first real computers were being built, artificial intelligence (AI) research suddenly received a tremendous boost. An American paper published in 1943 by McCulloch and Pitts (Warren McCulloch was a leading neurophysiologist, Walter Pitts a young mathematician) electrified science by offering a theory of the human brain which was based on the Turing machine. In Britain, the psychiatrist W. Ross Ashby published *Design For A Brain*. Those were heady times.

The optimism of those days was founded on the belief that the human brain and the computer operated on a very similar basis: that nerve cells behaved like gate circuits and therefore that a suitable combination of circuits would become an artificial brain. Gradually that dream turned sour: the picture painted by McCulloch and Pitts turned out to be a gross oversimplification of how brain cells really work; Ross Ashby and others did build machines that had some ability to learn and adapt, but nobody was prepared to call them artificial brains.

Soon a rival approach began to gain dominance. Some researchers had never been impressed by the desire to create an imitation brain; far better, they said, to concentrate on building a machine that behaved intelligently regardless of how it worked inside. The view which came to prevail, and still does among many AI workers, is that a machine is intelligent if it can do something that would be called intelligent when done by a human. In other words intelligence is what we find mentally difficult. Scratching your nose, adding two numbers together or recognizing yourself in the mirror involve mental processes but we can all do them so they are too simple to be called intelligent. On the other hand, playing a good game of chess, proving a geometry theorem or solving a problem in mathematical logic are beyond most of us and undeniably do demand intelligence. These, then, were the targets to aim for.

AI embraced these goals with enthusiasm. They coincided with the view that symbol manipulation was a good measure of intelligence and they fitted in with the mathematical background many AI researchers brought to their work. What is more, they were tidy activities with well-formulated rules which should be relatively easy to program into a machine. Success was close at hand. In January 1956 Herbert Simon announced to his students at Carnegie-Mellon University in Pittsburgh that he and Alan Newell had invented a thinking machine over the Christmas holidays.

He was right, they had. But there were no medals, no ceremonies, no outraged demonstrations in the streets; even the other participants at an AI conference later that year did not really seem overwhelmed. Newell and Simon were the first victims of 'it all depends on what you mean by intelligence', and it turns out that what people usually mean by intelligence is that which can be done by a person but not by a machine.

The Simon and Newell program was called Logic Theorist and it was designed to prove theorems in symbolic logic, an activity normally restricted to a fairly small number of mathematical philosophers who are, of course, highly intelligent. Logic Theorist could not only prove these theorems but, in at least one case, it found a neater proof than the best human minds had managed to produce. The great philosopher Bertrand Russell wrote to congratulate it on the improvement it had made to one of his proofs, but a philosophical journal refused to accept a paper describing the discovery and giving Logic Theorist as co-author. Yet its achievement was no rote learning but genuine intellectual originality. Outside this specialized field there was little interest; few people have a burning passion for symbolic logic and the response tends to be, 'if it can be done by a machine then it cannot have been as difficult as was made out'.

This attitude has haunted AI ever since; one by one each demonstration of intelligence somehow came to seem less intelligent when computers learned to do it. It happened to the programs that play chess (they cannot be intelligent, after all you can buy them now in almost any toy shop); it happened also to the programs that can do algebra; and even to those that make light work of the IQ tests we are still submitted to. Even within the computer world many people scorn the attempts to create intelligent programs.

The reasons should not be difficult to find. There is the obvious threat of losing our supremacy in an area which we tend to value very highly. (Computers could beat us from the very beginning at arithmetic, but then that has never had a very high status in our society – people who would die of shame if they had to announce that they are illiterate will proudly boast that they could never do long division.) But there is also a widespread feeling that true intelligence ought not to be something that can be specified in terms of rules and instructions but must rely on intuition, flair and imagination (whatever they may be) at least as much as on hard reasoning. Finally, and perhaps most importantly, is the feeling that intelligence must be versatile. We would be very doubtful of a person who can easily solve problems in geometry but is a total moron in every other respect. Even being able to chat about the weather or laugh at a joke, which may not in themselves be highly intelligent activities, provide a context for intelligence. Perhaps it is only when computer programs can do the same that there will be a general recognition of their intelligence.

But even if AI has failed to meet the challenge of producing a versatile computer program, one that can do many things intelligently, it has succeeded in creating programs which perform some specialized tasks in a way that we would certainly call intelligent in a person.

Big day at Monte Carlo
In July 1979, AI took to the stage in Monte Carlo, but somehow nothing turned out quite as expected. The opening appearance was certainly inauspicious. At the Monaco Summer Sports Palace the lights dimmed, the band struck up a suitably futuristic theme and a spotlight hit the stage to introduce the robot Gammonoid. The audience waited. The band played on. Nothing happened. The hapless machine had become entangled in the curtain and took five embarrassing minutes to extricate itself before finally appearing. If steel could blush! It was an unimpressive start.

But no matter, the audience had not come to see a robot mascot anyway; they had come to Monte Carlo for the much more serious purpose of watching the World Backgammon Championships. Over the next few days all eyes were focused on the world's leading players as they battled it out. Eventually, after a hard-fought contest, the trophy went to Luigi Villa of Italy. At 11 pm on the last day of the championship, the triumphant Villa sat down to fulfil his final commitment to the tournament: a $5000 winner-take-all match against a computer. The outcome was a foregone conclusion so not very many people stayed on to watch.

Luigi Villa playing backgammon with a robot in Monaco

Across the board from Villa stood Gammonoid, better behaved now, and poised ready to move its pieces. A telephone circuit linked the robot to its brains in Pittsburgh – a computer program called BKG 9.8 which had been written by Dr Hans Berliner of Carnegie-Mellon University. To demonstrate that there was no sleight of mechanical hand, an impartial official had been appointed to roll the robot's dice.

Play got off to a lively start. BKG had an early advantage in the first game and flexed its intellectual muscles with a shrewd move that chose short-term risk in return for long-term advantage. The gamble paid off and BKG took the first game. A very imaginative 'doubling' move in the second removed any remaining doubts that here was a player to be reckoned with. The news travelled fast and by the time that BKG was leading 5-0 the spectators' room was crowded. The next game made it 5-1 but brilliant defensive play, coupled with some lucky throws of the dice, took the computer to an overall 7-1 victory. Villa's pre-eminence had lasted only one day and Berliner was left the delicate task of consoling the defeated champion.

Since that day the moves have all been analysed and re-analysed by many expert players. There is no doubt that BKG 9.8 had better luck with the dice that night than Villa. And technically BKG was the poorer player: Berliner reports that, out of seventy-three moves where its choice was not forced by the game, the computer played eight in a less than perfect way whereas Villa's moves were almost all correct. But there is no disputing the imagination and brilliance of the computer's play; it may not have been perfect but it certainly had great style and insight.

The events of that Mediterranean night were a good indication of how far AI had matured since Alan Turing tried to program chess into a paper computer. And it was a victory that would have pleased Turing very much because he considered games of intellectual skill (chess and the Oriental game of go were his favourites) to be the ideal task for any computer that aspired to intelligence. Today's best programs can play chess very close to Grand Master level and can easily beat anyone at draughts (checkers), although they still struggle to play a decent game of go.

The reason why games have been so popular in AI studies is that they represent a closed world with fixed, unambiguous rules and a sufficiently large store of human expertise against which to judge the program's progress. What is more, there is plenty of scope for maneuver; as we saw when looking at expert systems, there are more options in a game of chess than any computer or any human brain could ever consider. The effect of this is to force some degree of intelligent judgment onto anyone or anything wanting to play the game effectively. And yet there are few people who would still maintain that playing a game, even one as difficult as go, is a demonstration of intelligent thought in the computer.

Easy thinking

At one time, playing chess or draughts or finding the proofs which Logic Theorist can tackle were the obvious choices for artificial intelligence. Few people can do them well so they have rarity value and being difficult they must be a higher achievement than easy thinking. But gradually this attitude began to alter so that today it could be said with only slight exaggeration that artificial intelligence is concerned with the easiest mental activities and not the hardest.

This is not a defeatist attitude that has settled for lower standards, but simply the realization that easy thinking is the most difficult. AI would give its collective right arm for a program that could understand and use the English language (or any other human tongue) as well as the average person can. A six-month-old baby has more ability to process and interpret visual information than any computer program can aspire to. And as for giving computers a sense of humor – nobody even knows where to begin.

This change of emphasis towards the commonplace activities of the mind has had a drastic effect on the role of AI. No longer is it the preserve of mathematicians and engineers wishing to make better computers (although that side is still there and very important) but now it is populated also by psychologists, philosophers and educators who have come into the subject for what computer techniques can reveal about the human brain. It may sound like a return to the days of McCulloch and Pitts and in fact AI has again become very much linked with neurophysiology, the study of the brain's structure and function.

He may not be able to read yet but even at this age a baby has more sophisticated sound and vision processing than any computer

The naïve assumptions have gone of course but, as we shall see, the old argument about whether AI should be trying to re-create the internal working of the brain, or simply the external appearance of intelligence, is as relevant as ever before.

The two pillars of this modern research are the study of visual perception and of language. Both are profoundly difficult in spite of, or perhaps because of, the fact that we can do them so easily. Because we have never had to think about how to see or how to understand language we are poorly placed for passing on these skills to a computer. Activities like chess and symbolic logic are much better worked out precisely because they do not come naturally to us. But even if AI has descended from the intellectual heights it once attacked there is little doubt that it is now facing a much harder task.

Understanding pictures

Look at the three drawings reproduced here: they are familiar enough visual tricks, but how does your brain actually work out what they mean? All three – the Penrose triangle, the devil's pitchfork and the Penrose stairs – can be instantly recognized as impossible objects: our brains do it very easily, but how could we set about programming a computer to see that they are visual frauds? Then again, are they as impossible as they seem? If so, how was it possible to draw them?

The Penrose triangle

Problems such as these, which deal with flat surfaces and straight edges, can now be successfully programmed into a computer but they are not nearly as simple as they may at first appear. The problem is one of converting a flat two-dimensional drawing into the three-dimensional object which our brains try to make of it. In 2D the picture may be perfectly reasonable but may not correspond to any reality in 3D. One way the computer can check this is to label all the edges as 'convex', 'concave' or 'occluding' (i.e. with one of the faces hidden). Because only certain combinations of edges can meet at a corner, it can work its way around the picture from edge to edge, labelling as it goes. When it has been over every one and returned to the first edge it should come up with the same label it started with; if not then the object cannot exist in 3D. The process works, but we cannot help but feel that our brains must have a simpler way of doing it.

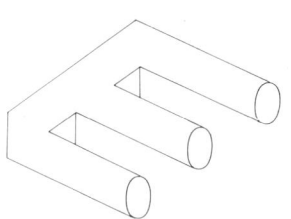

The devil's pitchfork

But even when there is no visual trickery involved, the process of recognizing and understanding the image being presented to our eyes is extremely difficult to explain. Once we move away from the neat world of straight lines there are immensely complex objects like faces, trees, landscapes, clouds, animals and cars which we somehow manage to identify – usually within about a tenth of a second. On top of this there are all the complexities of variable lighting, shadow, perspective, colour, texture and so on. There are also our vitally important abilities to see depth and movement. We understand very little of how our brains do all this and even less of how to program these skills into a computer.

OPPOSITE 'Ascending and Descending', lithograph by M.C. Escher – a striking use of the Penrose stairs

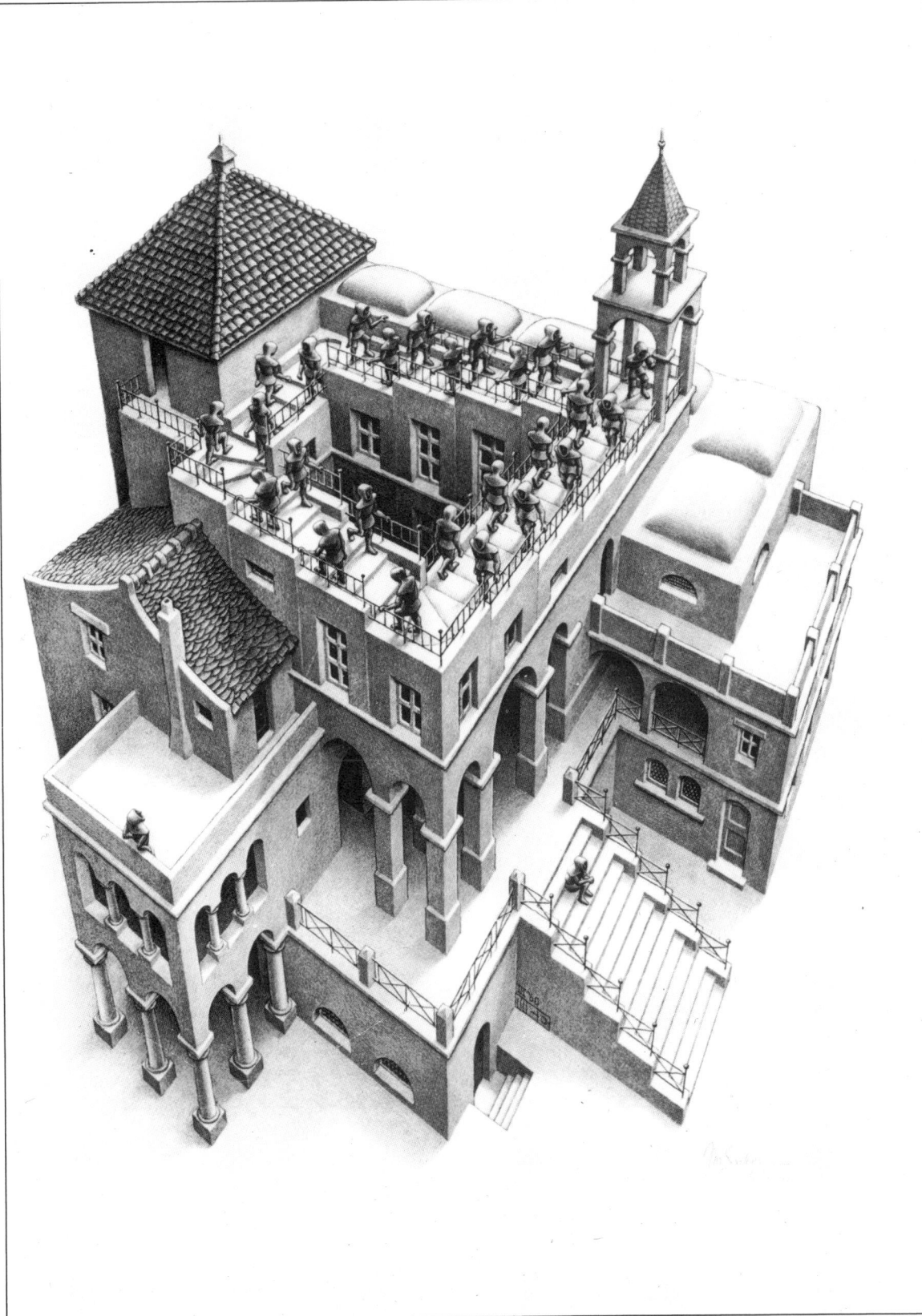

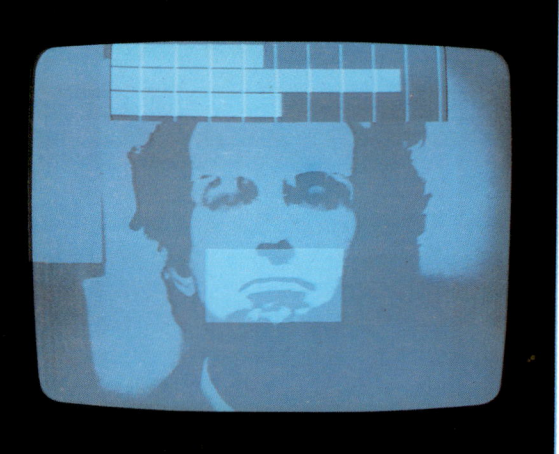

The WISARD image recognition system at Brunel University. At the front is its 'eye' – a TV camera; behind are the two racks of electronics which compare the scene with previously learnt patterns

Smiling and frowning. The three bars above the face show how strongly the computer identifies the image as a random pattern (top bar), a frown (middle bar) or a smile (lower bar). It clearly has no doubts in this case

But the problem we are faced with is even more subtle than it appears. At Brunel University in west London, researchers have produced a computer system called WISARD which can easily identify a familiar face regardless of its expression. Conversely, presented with several faces, it will identify which ones are smiling and which are not. Compared to conventional image recognition systems this is light years ahead. The problem is that, except in a very general way, we cannot explain how it recognizes a smile or a face. Its abilities come from inside itself rather than from an analysis of the object being viewed.

The approach used in WISARD is called 'bottom-up' design. It is fast, effective and very flexible, being able to work as easily with metal castings as with paper money or human expressions. But it offers no analysis of the scene it is viewing: it could recognize a devil's pitchfork but would not be able to work out what is wrong with it. The more common approach is called 'top-down'. It relies on analysis of the image and so allows more understanding of it, but is much slower and less flexible.

Top-downers start from the overall task and attempt to write a program that will perform it. What they are producing is programmed intelligence – algorithmic or heuristic techniques which are designed to achieve some result that is also produced by the brain. The program may, of course, be quite different from the pattern of mental events, but it can nevertheless provide valuable information about what is necessary and what is impossible in a particular process. For example, if a program that is designed to interpret a three-dimensional object from a two-dimensional drawing gives ambiguous results it might be quickly ruled out as inadequate. But if its failure corresponds to a known optical illusion, it may be a useful experimental tool for investigating the reasons why we sometimes get confused.

The vast majority of AI research makes use of this top-down approach to programmed intelligence. It is particularly effective in well-defined problem areas such as game playing, but even in the study of visual perception it has produced many important findings. One of the most influential researchers in this field, the British neurophysiologist David Marr, worked almost entirely with computers yet his ideas now form the foundation for much of the present knowledge about visual processes in the brain.

Bottom-uppers begin from a totally different position. They point to the fact that the brain is organized as a vast structure of neurons each of which is interconnected to as many as several thousand others. Whatever is going on in this network is obviously a very highly parallel process, quite different from the workings of any normal computer. To try to mimic such activity with a sequential program would be a hopeless task; instead they ignore the details of what is happening and aim to imitate the complexity of the structure. Its behavior may be difficult to predict in detail but it can be made to respond very intelligently.

In the case of the WISARD system, the pattern of light and dark in a television image is used to select addresses (locations) in a large randomly arranged array of computer memory. The system can be taught by showing it an object and storing a 1 in each location it has selected. Next time it is shown something, a simple count of the number of 1s that have been selected will indicate whether it is seeing exactly the same item as before or, if not, how similar the two objects are. With the addition of some further techniques the device can recognize faces with remarkable accuracy, quite untroubled by changes of expression.

The pattern of 1s and 0s stored in its memory is directly related to the image it is seeing, but not in any pre-planned fashion which allows us to say that it is comparing the size of the mouth or the height of the hairline. It would only be by examining the precise detail of its internal random wiring that we could ever find out how the pattern in memory relates to the picture on the screen. But there is really no need for us to know; two separate machines might be wired quite differently and yet perform equally well.

For the moment this is the choice we have to make: between top-down machines, which are designed to interpret specific features, and bottom-up machines, which recognize overall patterns. But the two techniques are certainly not mutually exclusive – it is likely that our brains make use of both and that any sophisticated computer vision system will eventually need to do the same.

Essentially the problem that looms over all attempts at computer vision is one of sheer volume of information. The richness of detail that we can see, and need to see, makes even the best computer systems seem pathetic by comparison. But when it comes to language, the other great aim of artificial intelligence, the difficulty is rather different. The rate at which information arrives is fairly manageable; the difficulty is in coping with the extraordinary complexity of rules we have devised for it.

Understanding words
The early history of computing is littered with shattered dreams of automatic translation. Perhaps the stories of 'the spirit is willing but the flesh is weak' becoming 'the vodka is good but the meat is bad' and 'hydraulic ram' being translated as 'water sheep' are, after all, apocryphal – but they reflect a genuine difficulty. The truth is that we all manage to cope with language so easily that we hardly notice its inconsistencies, but computers have a very hard time of it. If we are to get anywhere near the aims of the fifth generation, which include building computers able to communicate entirely through natural language, then we shall need to make rapid progress.

In broad terms, natural language programs deal with two main aspects of language: syntax, the structure and grammar of a statement; and semantics, its underlying meaning. Without syntax language can become a meaningless jumble of words, but semantics are what it is actually all about. In some way that nobody yet understands we manage to interpret language by combining an understanding of both these aspects. And yet we are also flexible enough to allow for the fact that much of language, especially spoken language, is ungrammatical and carries several layers of meaning within it. In order to be fluent, computers will have to cope with all of this, but for the moment most programs opt for one or the other – syntax or semantics.

There are, for example, several commercially available programs that allow a large database of information to be searched in response to requests in plain English. One very successful program of this type relies on a thorough knowledge of English grammar to analyse the structure of the sentence and then uses an internal dictionary to interpret each word. Once the meaning has been understood it handles the job of getting the required information out of the datastore. A similar technique is the basis of British research work currently under way at the Univesity of Lancaster; this aims to produce a program that will automatically attach a grammatical tag (noun, verb, adjective, etc.) to each word by analysing the syntax of the sentence. Its success rate is already very high but, of course, analysis is only a part of understanding vital information.

At the opposite end of the scale is an approach developed at Yale University. This technique ignores syntax almost completely and concentrates on getting directly to the meaning by categorizing words according to a number of basic concepts. For example: possessing something, causing something to happen, moving something and so on. Combined with an expert system containing knowledge about the relevant subject, these programs have also proved very useful in helping people to extract information from a databank. In one of the large oil companies, for example, a program of this type accepts questions in plain English, searches for the required information and automatically converts it into maps of the oilfield.

Although natural language programs, just like expert systems, are already very successful in narrow areas, we are still a long way away from computer programs that can understand all of a language including its slang, idiom and metaphor. A conversational machine, even one that only chatted about the weather or what was on television last night, would be a singular achievement. At least it would if it did so with understanding.

Consider the following conversation between a young woman and her therapist:

Young woman: Men are all alike!
Therapist: In what way?
YW: They're always bugging us about something or other.
T: Can you think of a specific example?
YW: Well, my boyfriend made me come here.

T: Your boyfriend made you come here?
YW: He says I'm depressed much of the time.
T: I am sorry to hear you are depressed.
YW: It's true. I am unhappy.
T: Do you think coming here will help you not to be unhappy?
YW: I need some help, that much seems certain.
T: What would it mean to you if you got some help?
YW: Perhaps I could learn to get along with my mother.
T: Tell me more about your family.
YW: My mother takes care of me.
T: Who else in your family takes care of you?
YW: My father.
T: Your father?
YW: You are like my father in some ways.
T: What resemblance do you see?
YW: You are not very aggressive but I think you don't want me to notice that.
T: What makes you think I am not very aggressive?
YW: You don't argue with me.
T: Why do you think I don't argue with you?
YW: You are afraid of me.
T: Does it please you to believe I am afraid of you?
YW: My father is afraid of everybody.
T: What else comes to mind when you think of your father?
YW: Bullies.
T: Does that have anything to do with the fact that your boyfriend made you come here?

The 'therapist' was in fact a computer, programmed to play the role of a psychotherapist of the Rogerian school – gently encouraging the patient to bring her fears and feelings out into the open and reflecting them back to her.

It is impossible to read through that dialogue without thinking that in some real sense the computer understands what is being said to it. It certainly manages some apparent flashes of insight, like the final remark, but in fact it is a fairly simple and quite unintelligent program with a script of prepared sentences into which it slots the appropriate nouns and verbs. When stuck for a response it can simply fall back on repeating what was just said to it, or asking a bland question like 'Tell me more about . . .'; and yet the program has a quite uncanny ability to convince people that it is human in its understanding. There are stories of hard-bitten computer engineers secretly discussing their emotional problems with it and of people coming unawares to it and believing that they were dealing with a person.

The program is called ELIZA and it was written by Dr Joseph Weizenbaum, a computer scientist at the Massachusetts Institute of Technology. It works by recognizing certain keywords in what is typed in, applying rules that transform the sentence in various ways, and using a script of prepared sentence types to produce its response. Basic transformations such as changing 'I' into 'you' and 'you' into 'me' are auto-

THINKCHIPS   69

Casual conversation at a party – ELIZA would be in its element here

matically carried out. There is sufficient flexibility in ELIZA for it not necessarily to give the same response to the same statement each time.

Weizenbaum was interested in examining the ways in which we often use language to disguise a lack of interest or understanding. It is an ability that comes in very useful, for example, when you are stuck with a boring companion at a party. One part of your brain keeps up a polite imitation of interest while the rest of your attention listens to the juicier discussion next to you or scours the room for a more welcome face. ELIZA can do this trick with great skill and can chat away for hours on end about any subject under the sun. But for the illusion to hold there must be at least an unconscious willingness to play along with it: there is no point in asking ELIZA to explain what it appears to be saying.

The effectiveness of ELIZA's tricks has led to some very important arguments about the ethics of computing and artificial intelligence and has prompted Joseph Weizenbaum to assert that there are certain areas of activity into which computers should never again be allowed to enter. We shall turn to look at these issues in the final chapter; but it is, in the meantime, an interesting reflection on our relationship with AI that one of the only programs that genuinely manages to convince many people of its intelligence is not and was never intended to be intelligent.

MOL 1
MOL 2
MOL 1+2
ROT X
ROT Y
ROT Z
TRANS X
TRANS Y
TRANS Z
ZOOM
SLAB
PERSP
RESET
BLINK
ERASE
ER-LABEL
ER-BONDS
POINTS
NET
ALL
ACIDIC
BASIC
H-ACCEPT
H-DONOR
LABELS
BONDS
COMPARE
DOCK
PLOT
CHAT
END

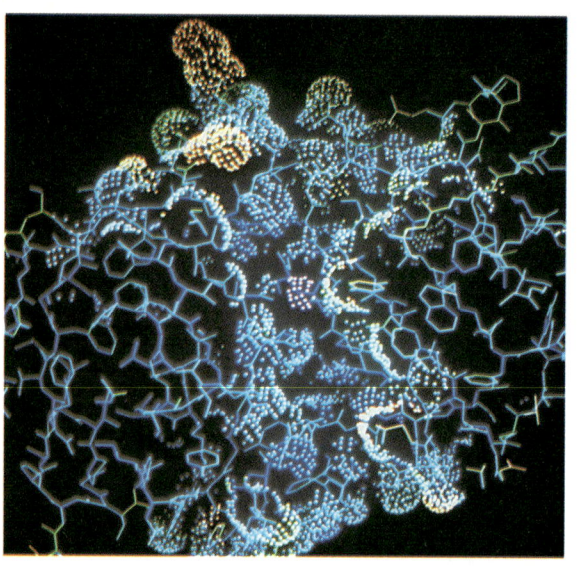

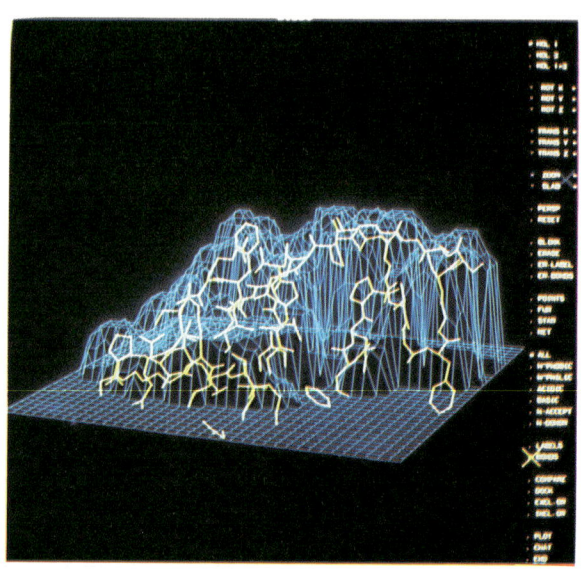

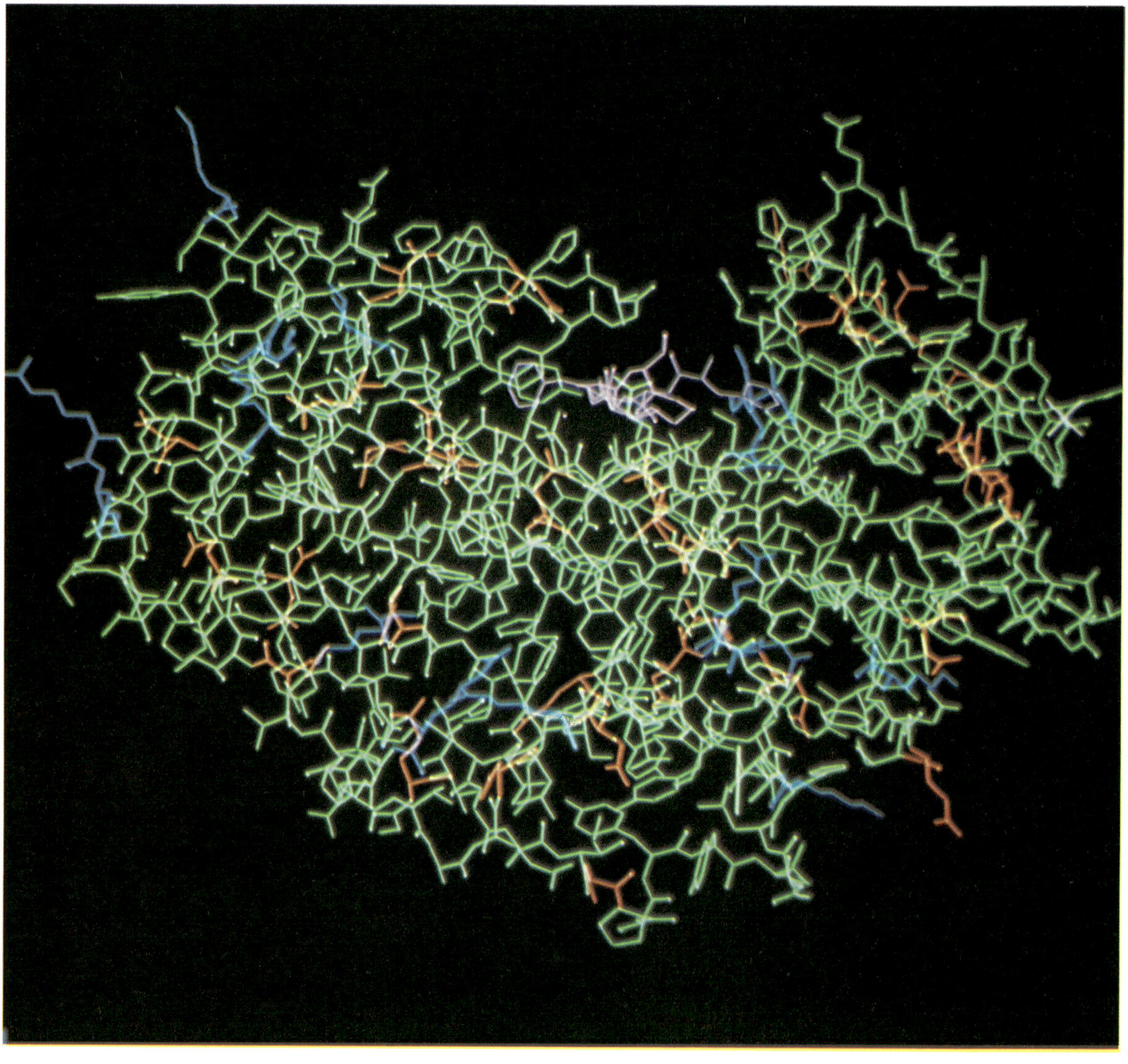

CHAPTER FIVE
Face to Interface

The first thirty years of computer history were largely devoted to making things easy for the new technology. In those days, computer users took it for granted that they would have to learn the complicated codes and programming languages demanded by the machines. Designing programs required a great deal of skill in manipulating the data into an easily digested form, then squeezing it into the tiny amounts of available memory and interweaving the actual processing with the slow and clumsy business of getting information in and out of the machine. The secret of success was to make the machine's interaction with us as convenient as possible for the machine.

It is only in very recent years that we have become more demanding and started to insist that computers should fit in with our needs. Progress has been rapid: it would have been unimaginable twenty years ago that computers could be as easy to use as they have now become and yet, compared to what lies ahead, we have hardly begun to change this relationship called the 'man–machine interface'.

Imagine the difference it would make if we never again had to sit tapping away at a keyboard but could simply talk to the computer about what we required – not just single words of command but a proper conversation about the task in hand. We would be able to show it scribbled notes or diagrams to explain what we were asking, and when the computer had finished its job, it could tell us its findings, show us a picture, write a description or keep quiet if it saw that we were busy.

Such sophistication is at least twenty years away and will depend as much on developments in psychology as in engineering – understanding language and pictures is, as we saw in Chapter Four, very much a part of the artificial intelligence effort. But even if truly intelligent communication is a long way away, there is still an enormous amount to be done with clever ignorance. Simply to have a machine that could convert spoken words into written ones – a dictation typewriter – would be quite an achievement even if it had no way of knowing what the words were about. On the visual side, the ability that computers now have to manipulate images according to the laws of space and optics has had a revolutionary effect on areas as far apart as the development of drugs and the production of cartoon feature films. It makes no difference, for the moment, that no computer shares our ability to look at a cartoon animal and decide whether its expression is happy or sad.

Enough to make your blood pressure rise

There is a small darkened room at Birkbeck College, London, where at most times of the day (and sometimes into the night) biochemists, pharmacists and crystallographers are to be found; they seem not to notice the stale, warm air and the ceaseless whine of fans and computer memory disks. Dominating the center of the room is a black box, rather like an overgrown TV set; on its screen tangles of multi-colored lines twist slowly round or rock gently from side to side. In this unearthly

OPPOSITE

ABOVE LEFT A pepsin enzyme molecule drawn by computer. The dotted areas indicate the surface of a deep cleft which cuts into one side of the molecule – this is the active region whose precise structure and shape determine the molecule's chemical activity

ABOVE RIGHT Mapping the shape of a complex molecule. The computer has drawn the 3D structure of a large molecule then thrown a net over it to produce a relief map of the structure. Techniques such as this are an essential feature of plans to design drugs and vaccines with computer graphics

BELOW The structure of the renin molecule. Its intricate three dimensional layout was only discovered through the use of very advanced computer graphics. The active region which drug companies are seeking to match is in the cleft at the top of the picture

place they search for ideas about how to make new drugs and industrial chemicals, they study how chemical processes within the body work and, occasionally, they stop just to gaze at the hypnotic patterns.

The pictures on the screen are molecular graphics: the computer age equivalent of the ball-and-stick models chemists of an earlier generation used to build. By dint of clever programming, the shapes appear to float within the screen, fully three-dimensional – the nearest atoms bright and almost jutting through the glass, the furthest dimmer and diminished by perspective. Propel the image towards you and it is possible to fly through the centre of a hormone molecule, its intricate structure sweeping past on all sides. Or, with a little more care, you can walk down the vast helical stairway of a DNA molecule, reading the genetic code as you go. It is a captivating experience but with a far more important role than that of intellectual video game.

The computer's ability to put chemists inside a molecule they are studying, to let them turn it around and sail through its inlets and canyons, does literally open up a new way of seeing things. The sort of chemistry that living organisms, such as we, make use of is based on enormously large and intricate molecules whose operation depends not just on certain groups of atoms being present in the molecule but also on how accessible they are in its tangled structure. The analogy so often used – but it is a good one – is of a lock and key, a protruding part of one molecule fitting snugly into the folds of another and only then being able to interact chemically with it. This lock-and-key approach is used by most of the large molecules within us, such as the enzymes, hormones, antibodies and so on. It ensures that, within the complex soup of a living cell, only those things that are meant to react together do so. It also imposes severe demands on the pharmacologists who must produce drugs, vaccines, etc. because in order to work, their chemicals, too, must have the required shape. Using computer graphics is virtually the only way of seeing these problems clearly.

It has, in fact, been one of the great success stories of computing. Until recently only a few forward-looking people, scattered through various universities and pharmaceutical companies, had any real interest in using computer graphics for drug design. Today enormous sums are being invested by all the big drug companies into graphics equipment and the expertise needed to make use of it.

One of the early successes, which helped to encourage this move, came from that computer room at Birkbeck College. The researchers there were interested in a natural substance called renin. Renin is one link in a chain of reactions which convert the hormone angiotensin into a form that makes blood vessels constrict and thereby increases the blood pressure. Normally this is used to adjust blood pressure to the correct level but some people suffer from chronic high blood pressure and, for them, blocking this chain would be an effective way to lower it. It was known that, for various reasons, renin was the most suitable link in the chain to try to attack, but there was no easy way of knowing how to set about it without having an idea of its shape.

What was needed was a dummy molecular 'key' designed to fit snugly into the cavity in the renin molecule. With this in place the renin would be, in effect, clogged up and unable to take part in its normal reaction. By a complex procedure the researchers were able to find the sequence of amino acid building blocks out of which the renin molecule is constructed. Then, by comparing it to other proteins, they were able to predict how the various sections of the molecule would be angled relative to their neighbors, and then to program it into a computer which produced a complete three-dimensional display of the whole molecule.

The pharmaceutical companies who bought this information are now racing to produce a drug that will block renin. It is not only shape they need to be concerned about: the successful drug must have the correct chemical qualities and, of course, it must not produce any unwanted side effects; but getting a good fit has to be the first step and it is one where the drug designers, too, will be using computer graphics in order to try out their prototype drugs, even before any new chemicals have been produced.

The rapid growth of molecular graphics is already taking it into many other areas. It is believed, for example, that vaccines could be safer and more effective if they were made artificially rather than from actual viruses. But the synthetic vaccines will only succeed in boosting the body's immunity if they mimic precisely the shapes of certain viral molecules. Then again, the finest filters known to science are substances called zeolites, which contain pores tiny enough to separate out individual molecules. They have enormous potential as industrial catalysts, but their development does depend on knowing how the size and shape of the pore relates to the molecules it is working with. Computer graphics are being actively used in both these areas and new vaccines as well as catalysts for the chemical industry are now being tested.

The point to notice about all this is that it has not required any new techniques of chemistry – the information that was needed was available, or could have been obtained, without computer graphics. But by opening up a new channel of communication between ourselves and the computer, we have enormously amplified the value of that information so that a list of numbers and symbols has now become a major source of inspiration.

From the computer point of view, molecular graphics make quite heavy demands: to show a large molecule rotating smoothly may involve recalculating the positions in space of anything up to 1000 or more points, 30 times every second. But compared to some of the applications that computer graphics are now entering, this is really quite trivial.

Picture power
There is one simple underlying reason why it has taken so long for computers to begin communicating effectively through pictures - the sheer volume of information involved. Consider the contents of this book. To store all of the text in a computer memory requires about 350,000 of the 8-bit 'words' that many microcomputers work with. But to store even a single one of the color illustrations would take up at least three times as much memory space.

The usual way of representing pictures within a computer is to divide them up into a large number of tiny squares called pixels or picture elements. Each pixel is assigned a number which specifies its color and brightness. The smaller the pixels, the more of them there are and the more detailed the picture becomes, but at the same time it takes more memory to store it and more processing time to do anything with it. Similarly, having many shades of color demands that each pixel must have a longer number associated with it than if the choice were just black and white.

There is no way of avoiding this problem, although it can be made smaller. For example, line drawings can be broken down into straight line segments and stored as lists of endpoints without having to record every intermediate point along the line or any of the background. The molecular pictures shown in this book were produced by this technique: it is usually called vector graphics. But if the need is for pictures with solid color and shading rather than just outlines, then the only recourse is to use so-called raster graphics in which every pixel is specified and scanned to produce a complete image. Given enough time and computer power it is possible to produce remarkably detailed pictures in this way.

Only a few years ago trainee pilots, learning their skills in a flight simulator, saw through the cockpit window a large-scale model of the airport they were approaching. As the aircraft moved in response to the pilot's actions, so a TV camera mounted on a large remotely controlled gantry 'flew' over the model. Special safety devices were needed so that a misjudged landing would not plough the camera into the expensive landscape. Today this vast assembly of machinery is defunct, replaced by computer graphics which can not only be programmed to show any airport we desire, but also at any time of day or night in any weather conditions.

Simulation has been a major driving force behind computer graphics. It is used not only for aircraft, including helicopters, but also for ships, cars, the NASA Space Shuttle and even town planning: it is cheaper to drive through a simulation of a proposed street junction than it is to build it first and only then discover a blind spot in the middle lane. Not surprisingly, the military has taken a great interest in computer simulation and can use it now to train anyone from a tank commander preparing for battle to an undercover agent about to enter an unfamiliar city.

ABOVE The biggest computer game of them all. This Boeing 737 is a flight simulator – computers make it respond like the real aeroplane in every detail. They also produce the graphics display which is seen through the window, examples of which are shown below

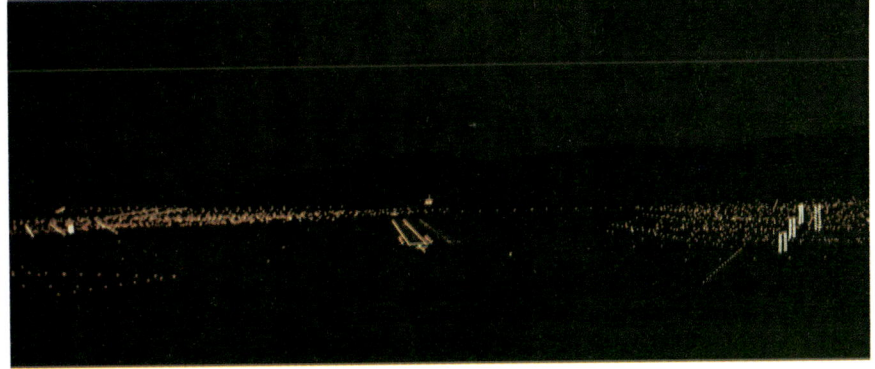

Approaching Hong Kong on a clear night

Touchdown on Runway 5 Left at Taipei on a misty night

To be effective, simulation demands very sophisticated computer processing. It is not just a question of producing detailed pictures; those pictures must move and change as we alter our position and must do so in ways that obey the laws of physical space and of light. Imagine driving through a simulated street scene including buildings, trees and other vehicles. As our viewpoint changes, trees by the road will seem to move past faster than the more distant buildings, objects will appear to change their shape as we see them from different angles and some things, like the other vehicles, will be moving independently within our field of view. To allow for every one of our possible viewpoints the computer must contain information about all sides of a building; but it must also know that buildings are not transparent and so work out which parts are visible and which are hidden at any moment. It is a brain-curdling exercise in three-dimensional geometry, yet it must be done over and over again so rapidly that, like the separate frames of a movie film, it blends into smooth motion.

Simulation equipment has always been extremely expensive. Yet, as computer technology becomes ever cheaper, many people in the simulation industry are looking towards a business boom based on home simulation. If you have ever longed for an opportunity to brave the Cresta run, fly an air–sea rescue helicopter or drive through Paris on the wrong side of the road, then you probably have no more than ten years to wait before computing lets you do it.

It is the need for animation at a rate of 25 or 30 frames per second that sets a limit to how much detail computer simulation can include. Paradoxically, the one application of computer-generated images in which rapid redrawing has not been allowed to restrict picture complexity is computer animation – the production of cartoon films and film special effects. It has been known to take months to program a single frame and minutes of computer processing time just to draw it. It is, for the moment, the ultimate application of painting by numbers.

Traditionally, animated cartoons have been produced by drawing them on sheets of transparent plastic called cels, one for the background, one or more for each character, and others for objects that may need to be moved. In this way successive frames showing a movement could be laid over the other cels without having to redraw everything for each frame. By arranging the layering of the cels it is possible to make a character pass in front of some objects and behind others. Certain frames, often at the start and end of a movement or where a special expression is required, are called key frames and drawn by the most experienced artist. These are the frames that maintain the identity of the character throughout the film. The frames in between the key frames are drawn by an 'in-betweener', a junior artist.

The whole process is extremely slow, very labor-intensive and, for the most part, uninteresting. It was a natural candidate for computeriza-

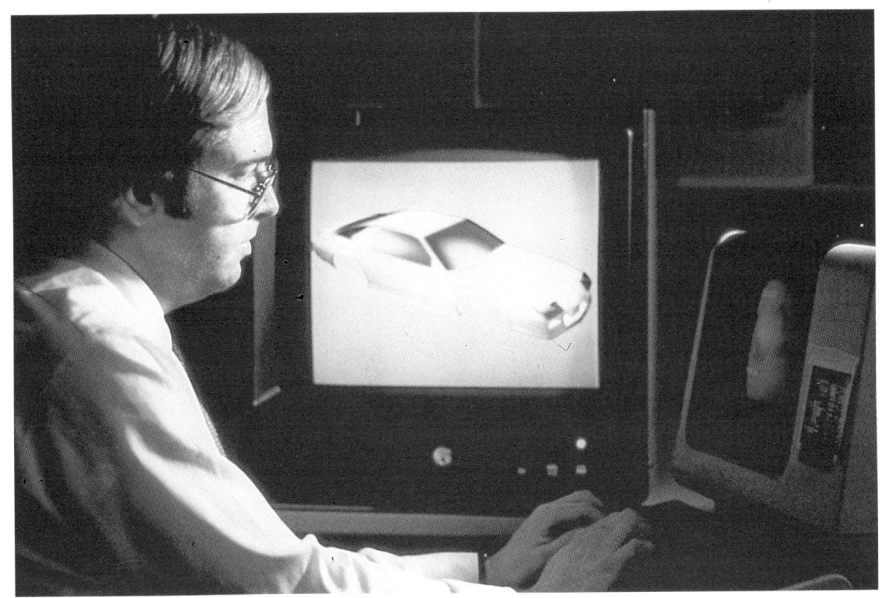

Computer graphics are widely used in car design because they allow the finished product to be seen from all angles even before the first mock-up is built. This is a Chevrolet Camaro

tion. Whole feature films like *Tron*, for example, and special effects sequences like those in *Star Wars* are now being made with the help of computers. Of course, the creative part – actually thinking up how it should look – is done by the artists; what the computer can do is to remove the drudgery.

There are programs that can take two frames and automatically 'in-between' them over any specified number of intermediate frames. It is even possible to program repetitive movements so that a character can be made to walk realistically for as long as we need. By superimposing several separate picture planes one on top of another, we can reproduce the effect of cels so that background and foreground can be altered independently. But perhaps the most important contribution of computing has been not simply to reproduce the traditional methods, but to offer cartoon animation access to the sort of three-dimensional mathematics that the best simulations can make use of.

Imagine a typical scene: a room with a fire blazing in the hearth and a candle on the table; the door bursts open letting in a blast of wind which flares up the fire and blows out the candle; the villain enters. As the flames flicker, areas of light and shadow throughout the room will be constantly changing. The door, as it opens, will perhaps move into shadow but catch the light along its edge. Some objects, like the table top, have a matt texture; others, a brass doorknob for example, are shiny and so will catch highlights from the flickering light. Suddenly, as the candle gutters, all the lighting changes. We see a reflection of the villain's face in a mirror above the fire; he turns his head to the right – which way does the reflection turn?

Like the simulation program, an animation like this is essentially an exercise in optics and three-dimensional geometry. But unlike the simulation, which has to respond in real time to the trainee's actions, cartoon animation can be filmed one frame at a time and so can apply a lot more computing power to each picture. Such programs are now

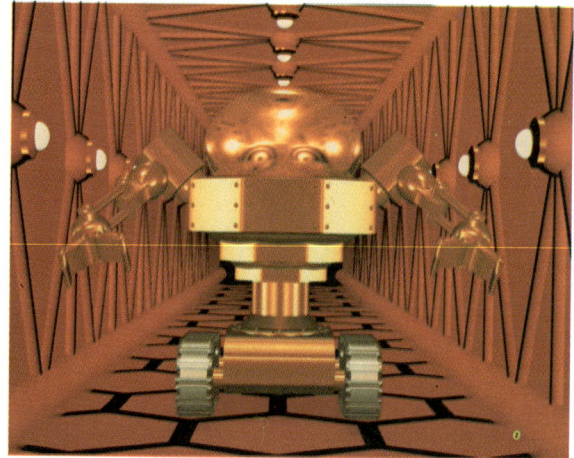 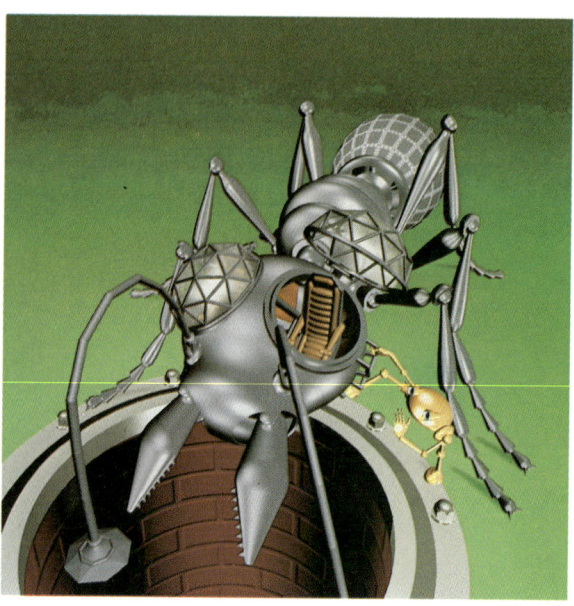

'Panzer' and 'Ant Farm' – two stills from The Works, an animated film produced by the New York Institute of Technology's Computer Graphics Laboratory. Although unfinished, The Works is generally acknowledged to be the most impressive example ever of computer graphics animation

being tried out by some of the leading animation companies for precisely this sort of work – looking after the intricacies of physical space, perspective and light, while the artist concentrates on developing the characterization. The computer will even work out the reflections in a mirror and how they must appear to move.

Advanced graphics programs like these can simulate almost any color, texture or lighting and they will show whatever movement we require, either of the object or of our viewpoint. But they can only do this for an image that has already been created by the artist. For example, once all aspects of a car have been entered into the computer it can look at it from any angle, change its color and so on but it cannot create a suitable car to begin with. We could, of course, store several designs in the computer and simply ask for a red no. 5; but each time we get a no. 5 it will be exactly the same design of car. Because the computer does not have any general notion of 'car', 'face', 'desert landscape' or whatever, it means that the shapes and arrangements of objects must be put in by us.

Imagine how much easier it would be if we could just say to the computer: 'I want a hilly landscape with a stream in the foreground and snow on top of the hills, put grass everywhere else and a few bushes. Oh, and while you're at it, stick some pine trees up on the hills.' Well, we can.

The land that never was
A few years ago a Swiss mathematician called Benoit Mandelbrot posed a question of breathtaking simplicity: 'How long is the coast of Britain?' This question, and the answer he provided, have had an astonishing impact. Already, they have led to a whole new branch of geometry, provided insight into such apparently unconnected topics as the stability of oil rigs, the growth and pattern of blood vessels, the shape of galaxies and price fluctuations on the stockmarket; and they have also created some of the most stunning computer graphics ever produced.

Fractal Planetrise by Benoit Mandelbrot. Standing on a non-existant moon we watch an Earth that never was. Both worlds are a figment of fractals and the computer's imagination

Point Reyes, probably the most complex computer image created so far. It was produced at Lucasfilm and makes use of fractals as well as special technqiues for producing textures, shadows, reflections and natural looking vegetation. This is the kind of realism which we may expect to see in films within a couple of years

Mandelbrot's question is important because it has no simple answer. The length of any coastline depends on the scale at which you measure it: if the measuring stick is 50 miles long you will get one figure; do the same with a 1-mile stick and the bays and headlands you missed before will lead to a much greater result. As the measuring rod gets shorter so you will pick up smaller features, eventually down to individual boulders, rocks and pebbles. By the time you are measuring around each grain of sand and grit the length of the coastline will have grown enormously.

It appears a trivial point, but Mandelbrot's purpose in raising it was to examine all of those things whose measurement depends on the scale at which you measure them. We could just as easily ask, 'What is the surface area of a cloud?' or, 'How uneven is a mountain?'; many naturally occurring shapes in landforms, plants and water have this property. Mandelbrot gave the phenomenon the name 'fractal' and went on to develop a mathematical way of dealing with it which has become known as fractal geometry. This in turn has led to a major breakthrough in computer graphics.

If you were shown a selection of irregular shapes you would be able to say fairly easily whether any of them looked convincingly like an island. Some might be too regular – nature does not on the whole display straight lines and right angles; others may be too irregular, like spidery inkblots. But somewhere in between will lie shapes just formless enough perhaps to be an island. The same is true of many other natural forms – intuitively we can judge whether a jagged line could be the silhouette of a mountain range or a curving line the course of a river. Because fractal geometry provides a mathematical way of defining shapes that are island-like, river-like, mountain-like and so on, it offers computers the ability to produce an endless number of totally convincing but quite unreal landscapes.

No longer does an artist painstakingly have to draw the landscape. The computer program can now create Alpine valleys, islands, rolling hills, deserts, whatever we want. Each one will be unique, original and perfectly realistic: fractal geometry defines them all.

Versatile though they are, fractals are largely restricted in computer animation to producing the large-scale features of landscape. On a smaller scale they are less applicable, but recent research has come up with a number of so-called stochastic techniques which use carefully controlled randomness to create a wide range of textures and shapes: fire, grass, running water and different kinds of trees and bushes, for example. Once again they rely on the fact that, while no two oak trees are the same, every oak tree is recognizably different from every pine tree. By programming in only the general factors that make a tree look like an oak rather than a pine, or give something the texture of grass rather than of gravel, it is now possible to produce amazingly realistic scenery.

Within the next year or two we shall be seeing feature films which make use of all these techniques to produce completely computer-created settings for cartoons and special effects sequences. But simpler kinds of fractal landscape have already been used: for example in the Death Star sequence of *Star Wars*. The two pictures shown on p.79 (one comes from Mandelbrot's laboratory at IBM, the other from Lucasfilm who produced the *Star Wars* graphics) show just what we can expect the computers to create for us.

This revolution in computer graphics (for it is nothing less than that) has only been going for a couple of years, fuelled by the falling price of computer power and the development of new programming techniques. Its effects are widespread: we have not even touched on areas such as architectural design, medical scanning and computer-aided design for engineering; all these are developing rapidly.

This explosive growth is having a profound effect on the way we use computers, not so much because it deals with new types of information but because it communicates information in a way our brains find particularly convenient. Computers, it must be remembered, are general-purpose machines: it makes no difference whether the pulses going through the processing unit represent pictures, numbers, musical notes, letters or parts in an automotive catalogue. It is quite immaterial, and many of the changes now taking place in computing have no effect at this level. They are far more concerned with the appallingly difficult problem of getting this information in and out of the machine in a useful form.

Pictures are particularly appropriate because our brains have evolved large and highly specialized regions specifically to deal with them, so this is a very efficient channel of communications. The other major form of communications we employ deals with sound, in particular, speech.

All too often we see only the trivial gimmickry of computer speech: cars, cameras, watches, calculators all with identical electronic voices and nothing of interest to say for themselves. But there is a more important side to it: computer hearing and computer speech are already bringing great benefit to many handicapped people and, when they are good enough, they could become a very widespread means of communicating with computers. Looking further ahead, some people believe that they may lead to the ultimate channel of communication – the telepathic computer.

Computerspeak
Language is to do with meaning and, as with computer pictures, the task of understanding this meaning is in the category of artificial intelligence. Speech on the other hand can be produced and recognized without any real understanding; it is simply a varying pattern of sounds and can be treated as nothing more than that. Again, as with pictures, it has been much easier to produce artificial speech than to recognize the

real thing. This is hardly surprising as the burden of work always falls on the listener. Our brains are clever enough to make sense of even the low-quality speech of a computer. Computers are less skilled and so find it much more difficult to recognize human speech unless it is spoken very clearly and without distractions.

The main difficulty with representing speech in a computer is that it does not break down into neatly separate sounds. Speech is a flowing, dynamic process in which every sound may be altered by what came before, what is coming next and what broader context it is contained within. For example, 'this' contains an 's', and so does 'summer', but say 'this summer' and you have extended the consonant 's' to link both words. How is a computer to know how to allocate that lengthened 's'?

On a broader scale, we alter the way that we say words in order to indicate the end of a sentence, or to show that we are asking a question. Whether we are angry or surprised, a Texan or a New Yorker, young or old, male or female – these and countless other factors affect the way that different people say a word and the way that the same person will say it at different times. Of course, there must be common features in every utterance of a particular word otherwise we would never recognize it, but defining them has proved harder than expected.

Both computer speech and computer voice recognition, such as they are, often tackle the job by dividing speech into phonemes – basic units of sound like 'th', 'a', 't'. To produce speech, a computer may be programmed with a dictionary of words and the sequence of phonemes needed to produce them. Speech recognition uses a reverse dictionary and looks for the closest match to the phoneme pattern it has detected. This simple technique lies behind most of the speech devices that are used in consumer products or available for home computers. The obvious limitation is that their vocabulary is restricted to those words available in the dictionary.

Probably the most valuable use of this simple and relatively cheap technology is to help disabled people. For someone who is paralysed everyday tasks like switching on a light, closing the curtains or dialling a telephone number may be physically impossible. Yet they are all things that can easily be controlled by a home computer using a speech-recognition device and a small vocabulary of commands. For blind people a speaking calculator or watch, just an irritating gimmick to the rest of us, can be a most valuable asset. Voice output is also proving useful in teaching Braille, by speaking each letter as it is pressed on the Braille machine. These are valuable applications which could easily be extended without the need for any technological breakthrough. But if the aim is to give computers truly human powers of speech and hearing then very much more needs to be done.

Sound is a vibration of the air which can be characterized by its amplitude (how strong the vibrations are) and its frequency (how rapid they are). In any complex sound like speech there may be many separate

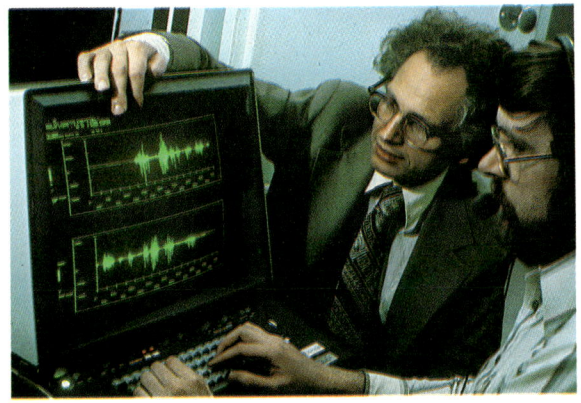 

LEFT A computer speech recognition system which can transcribe normal connected speech from a one thousand word vocabulary with 91% accuracy. By human standards this would be very poor but it is quite an achievement for computing

RIGHT This blind typist can check and correct all her own work by telling the computer to read it back to her. Its voice synthesiser will read it phonetically, spelling any words it cannot make sense of

frequencies of vibration simultaneously, each at a different amplitude. They combine together to produce the irregular fluctuations of air pressure that reach our ears. As the sound changes so this mixture alters, different frequencies becoming more or less prominent. One way of characterizing such sounds is to pick a short period of time, such that the sound does not have time to change very much, and measure the amplitude at a number of different frequencies. Some will be stronger than others and different sounds will show a different pattern with strong and weak amplitudes occurring at different frequencies. The central problem has been to find an efficient way of converting the vibrations picked up by a microphone into this sort of information about the mix of frequencies that makes up these vibrations.

There are numerous ways of doing this but the most promising, which has fairly recently been developed, goes by the name of linear predictive coding. It is highly mathematical but basically it works by combining the measure of a sound's overall amplitude at a number of earlier instants to predict the present amplitude. The combination that gives the correct prediction can be used directly to show how that sound breaks down into its mixture of different frequencies without any need actually to measure each of them. One of the main advantages of this approach is that it is particularly good at bringing out those features of speech sounds that are useful for recognition.

Another new technique, called dynamic programming, which helps this process considerably, is a means of allowing for the fact that a particular word will always contain the same sequence of sounds, but the timing of that sequence may vary quite widely. For example, the word 'table' will always begin with a 't' followed by the long 'ay' vowel and then a 'b', but the amount of time we spend on the vowel will vary each time we say it. This variation in timing makes it very difficult to match up an analysed sound with a stored 'template' that it must be compared to. Using dynamic programming it is now possible to squeeze and stretch the information in a way that will find the sequence regardless of timing.

With sophisticated techniques like these, the best of today's speech technology can achieve over 90 per cent accuracy when listening to normal connected speech with a limited vocabulary. This may be very impressive or very unimpressive according to your point of view, but it is certainly a long way away from human abilities. Perhaps the biggest problem with computer speech recognition is that we cannot expect to separate the mechanics of identifying a sound pattern from the interpretation of its meaning. Psychological research shows clearly that we take all sorts of shortcuts in listening to speech – in particular we use our knowledge of the topic under discussion and the preceding words to narrow down the possibilities for what we are about to hear. To that extent we hear what we want to hear.

Any computer system attempting to imitate these skills will also need to understand and make judgments about what it is hearing in order to search more efficiently through its knowledge of sound patterns. As with pictures, it is the vast quantity of information that overwhelms the imagination: the English language contains around 300,000 words, each of which involves a complex pattern of sound information. It would be impossible for any computer to search through that lot at the normal speaking rate of around five words per second. Early hopes that simple rules of grammar might help to narrow the search have proved unfounded; language is not that simple.

These problems are particularly acute for speech recogniton but they apply also to speech synthesis. To sound truly convincing, a computer will have to adjust the intonation of words according to their context, which means that to some extent at least it must know what it is talking about. Of all areas of computing, speech processing has probably proved the biggest disappointment because many people thought that it would be relatively easy. In fact the conversational computer is still a very long way away, but that should not detract from the value of what is possible.

There are many occasions when simple facts, warnings or commands are required and speech is the best medium of conveying them. Pilots, for example, face a number of hooters and horns to alert them to possible dangers; research suggests that spoken warnings could be more effective. There are various industrial processes, for example in photography, which need to be carried out in near or total darkness – speech would be a useful way of taking instrument readings or controlling equipment in these conditions. One application that is likely to grow as speech technology improves a bit further is for telephone access to a computer. Researchers at Bell Telephone Laboratories have produced a system which will answer queries about airline flights and accept bookings over the telephone. The same idea could be used for many kinds of enquiry and ordering service because a fairly restricted vocabulary will be sufficient to deal with most calls.

Essentially all speech processing is an attempt to extract the impor-

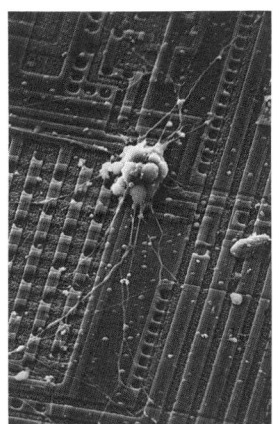

A nerve cell growing on the surface of a silicon chip (seen here through a scanning electron microscope). This is the forefront of experimental technology but it could one day lead to effective hybrids between computers and people

tant pattern of informaton out of a whole jumble of relevant and irrelevant sounds. The fact that we can do it, even when the speech is ungrammatical, full of 'ums' and 'ers' and heard against a background babble shows that it can be done. Eventually we are bound to crack the secret of how it is done. Extracting patterns from an apparently random mess of information is one of the central aspects of all computer communications. It applies just as much to recognizing a picture in which shadows or changes of colour and texture serve to confuse the simple outlines. But why stop there with the senses that we already have, why not create new ones?

Everything that we do or think or say is present within us as patterns of nerve signals and brain waves, mixed in, it is true, with all sorts of things we do not know about, but there nonetheless. What is to stop us decoding and using these signals directly? Some people already have artificial limbs controlled by the motor nerves which previously operated their natural ones. Recent research in San Francisco has shown that a computer can successfully decode the different brain waves which result from looking at various flashing lights and use these to enter commands into the computer.

Nobody is saying it would be easy (nor is speech recognition), but could we not think of interfacing the computer directly to the brain and central nervous system? If your reaction is to reject the idea, consider what it would mean for people with paralysis or speech impairment, or for the many severely spastic people who are imprisoned by their inability to communicate through words or actions. The brain-wave detector would only require a few skin electrodes on the head, just as when a doctor takes an electroencephalogram (EEG). With such a system, simple control of wheelchairs or other equipment could be achieved fairly easily. Given time it might be possible to develop the ultimate system of communication: a truly telepathic computer.

But it may be possible to go beyond even this by putting the computing circuitry inside the body. Research at the University of Warwick is looking into special silicon chips which can directly detect complex chemicals within a liquid. Initially these might have applications in biotechnology, for instance, later on as probes for medical monitoring, but there is every possibility that they could eventually be made to react to the chemical changes associated with nerve activity. Then there is a distant hope of implantable devices that could repair the effects of spinal injury or certain paralysing diseases by detecting nerve impulses, decoding and processing them, then sending appropriate signals to motor nerves or artificial aids. Because of the difficulty of making precise connection to individual nerves the computer chip would probably use a self-adapting program, which would in effect learn how to produce the correct responses. It is unlikely to happen before the end of the century but it is a perfectly serious expectation.

CHAPTER SIX
Silicon Cities

Across the Atlantic at the University of Durham scientists, gowned and masked like surgeons, work in elaborately controlled clean rooms. Their experiments are aimed at developing Langmuir-Blodgett films – perfectly arranged layers just a single molecule thick. In a research laboratory in New York State the surgical masks give way to padded gloves. Scientists there are working on Josephson junctions – tiny circuit elements which operate at temperatures near absolute zero. Elsewhere, proteins, bizarre new kinds of plastic and computers that have no physical existence at all are being studied.

In the past few years there has been an astonishing fanning out of scientific interest into new areas, all of it encouraged by one demand: the need to make computers faster and smaller. The truth is that computer technology in its present form is reaching the end of the road. Improvements are still possible, but there are fundamental limitations in the material from which chips are made that will not allow the gates to switch very much faster. Similarly, the existing technology for making chips cannot produce circuits that are significantly smaller than at present. Projects like the Fifth Generation computer and speech recognition depend on the development of new hardware technologies.

Some of the ideas now being floated will, if they succeed, completely change the way in which computers operate. But it is safe to make two broad generalizations about the foreseeable future. Firstly, that the majority of computers will remain as electronic machines and secondly, and more specifically, that they will make use of semiconductor electronics.

Neither one thing nor the other
In general, all materials can be divided into those that allow electricity to flow through them – the conductors, and those that do not – called insulators. Metals are always good conductors; typical insulators are glass, plastics and rubber. Semiconductors, as the name suggests, lie somewhere in between – neither conductor nor insulator. But the really useful thing about them is that their ability to conduct electricity can be dramatically affected by the presence of impurities. Combining regions with different types of impurity allows us to produce devices that can act as switches, changing from conductor to insulator and back again. These make up the gates which form the basic building blocks of all computers.

Any semiconductor, in order to work in this way, must be in the form of a crystal. To a physicist a crystal is a solid in which all of the atoms are arranged in an ordered regular pattern. This may produce a beautiful geometrical solid like quartz or the blue copper sulphate crystals of school chemistry experiments; but it does not have to. A shapeless lump will do just as well provided that the regular internal pattern is present throughout.

The atoms are held in place within this crystal lattice by bonds which

Operating under conditions of absolute cleanliness, this trough at the University of Durham is being used to deposit a Langmuir-Blodgett film. It is a technology which is likely to be of great importance to future chip development

The atoms are held in place within this crystal lattice by bonds which they establish with the adjacent atoms. The number and arrangement of these bonds depend on the atomic structure. All atoms consist of a positively charged nucleus surrounded by electrons, each of which carries a negative electric charge. The electrons are dispersed through a number of layers around the nucleus. The ones right on the outside, called the valence electrons, are the ones that interact to form bonds. Different types of atom have different numbers of valence electrons, between one and eight. Silicon, the most commonly used semiconductor, has four and so each silicon atom is able to make bonds to four others.

The role of the valence electrons, however, is not limited to making bonds. They are also directly involved in the conduction of electricity. An electric current is just a flow of electrons so, if a current is to flow through a material, there must be some mobile electrons within it. In any atom the inner electrons are the most firmly held by the nucleus so it is the outer, valence electrons that are most likely to provide the electron flow. In a metal there are always many electrons available for carrying a current, so metals are good conductors. Insulators, however, require very large amounts of energy for their valence electrons to break away, and so no current can flow. What about semiconductors? In a pure crystal of silicon all of the valence electrons are tied up but the energy required to free an electron is relatively small. So, even at room temperature, there is sufficient heat energy present to allow some of the electrons to move through the crystal. Hence pure silicon is a slight but very poor conductor.

Consider, though, what would happen if into this perfect crystal of silicon we were to introduce an impurity atom having, say, five valence electrons. Four of them would immediately form bonds to the adjacent silicon atoms, leaving one spare electron which is only loosely held and readily available for current flow. Adding just a tiny amount of such an impurity (the process is called doping) can have a great effect on the conductivity. It produces what is called an n-type semiconductor.

What if we go the other way and dope the crystal with a substance having only three valence electrons? All three of them form bonds but there is a hole where the fourth should be. Relative to the surrounding crystal the hole is a region of positive charge because a negatively charged electron is missing. Now the hole – and this needs a bit of thinking about – is not tied to that particular spot. Just like an electron it can flow through the crystal carrying, in this case, a positive current. Imagine a line of people holding buckets. Each of the buckets is full of water except for one, which is empty. It is a rule that you must fill an empty bucket which is in front of you. As each person in turn obeys the rule the hole in the chain moves steadily backwards, even though none of the buckets has changed hands.

In the same way, a hole can move through a semiconductor crystal. At each step it is filled by a nearby electron, creating a hole where that electron used to be. Semiconductors of this sort are called p-type, because the current is carried by positively charged holes. In the n-type semiconductor, negatively charged electrons form the current.

The ability to produce n-type and p-type materials is the essence of semiconductor technology. During the second generation computers were made up out of many thousands of individual components. There were transistors in which one electric current could be used to control another, resistors whose low conductivity could be used to set current and voltage levels within the circuit and diodes which allowed current to flow one way but not the other. Pure copper wire had to be used to join up these components because, being a very good conductor, it would not introduce unwanted effects of its own. Today all of this can be done within a single chip of crystalline silicon.

High levels of doping result in good conductivity, lower levels can produce the equivalent of resistors. The junction between a region of n-type and a region of p-type forms a diode. More complex patterns can produce many different types of transistor. There is no need to manufacture each component individually and no need to connect them up with bits of wire. The tricky part is making it all small enough.

Sharpening the pencil
It is very difficult to give any realistic impression of the complexity involved, simply because nothing else man-made has ever been so intricate. But, as a rough guide, a typical fairly complex chip, like a microprocessor, involves about as much detail as two complete street maps of the whole of London – all squeezed into a few square millimeters. In fact the problems of laying out an integrated circuit are very much like those involved in urban planning. It is very easy, for example, to get your main communications routes neatly laid out but much harder to make sure that each district has proper access to them. Like buildings, individual circuit elements within a chip need to have power supplied to them, but threading gas pipelines, power cables and water mains through a densely built-up city is a planners' nightmare. So it is for the chip designer who must weave power and signal paths through the silicon landscape. (See title page illustrations.)

The process of laying out this complex pattern begins as a series of very large precision drawings which represent the various layers within the chip. They show all the n-type and p-type material, the insulating regions and the interconnections. On anything but the simplest chips, the drawings are so complex that no human designer could ever hope to grasp them unaided. Powerful computers are needed to handle much of the routine of laying out individual elements and checking that everything is connected as it should be. When the drawings are complete and the computer is satisfied that the design will produce the required results, the process of transferring all of these patterns onto the silicon can begin.

 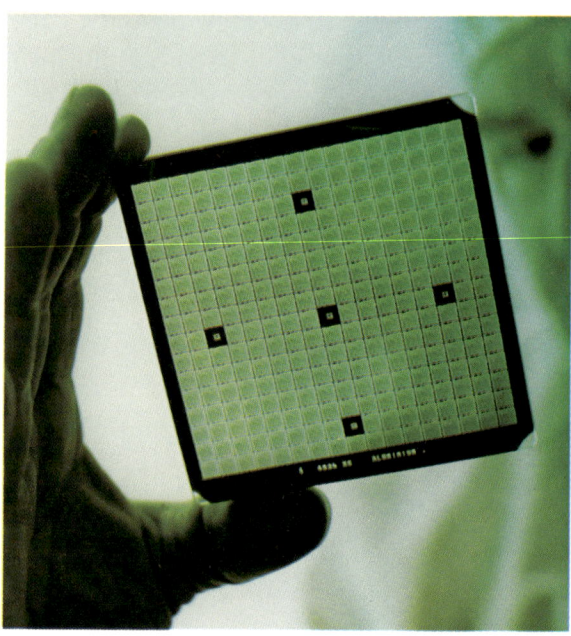

LEFT Putting the finishing touches to the master plan of a silicon chip mask

RIGHT Reduced in size and duplicated many times over, this mask will print its patterns onto a whole wafer of silicon in one exposure

In its present form this is essentially a photographic printing technique, called photolithography. It begins with a special camera, using very high-precision optics and operating under conditions of great cleanliness, which reduces the giant master drawings down to intricate miniatures called masks, the same size as the final chip is to be. Because the drawings represent different layers within the chip, it is essential that they must line up exactly, and complex precautions are needed to ensure accurate positioning and to avoid vibrations.

Chips are produced, several hundred at a time, on wafers of pure silicon. In order to translate the pattern of clear and dark areas on the mask into regions of doping in the chip the wafer is coated with a chemical called a photo-resist and light is projected onto it through the mask. The photo-resist reacts to light by setting solid; in those areas where the mask was dark it remains soft and can easily be washed away. So we can produce a pattern of exposed areas of silicon and protected areas covered by the hardened photo-resist. By stepping the wafer repeatedly under the projector the same pattern is repeated for every chip to be made on that wafer.

When a whole batch of wafers is ready they are placed into an oven, the air is removed and a gas containing the doping substance is fed in. Where the silicon is exposed it absorbs some of the dopant and by varying the time, gas concentration and so on a very precise level of doping can be achieved. The hardened photo-resist is then removed with a special solvent and the process starts again for the next layer. Using this one basic technique of photo-resist masking it is possible to carry out many different processes on the silicon. Apart from n-type and

SILICON CITIES 91

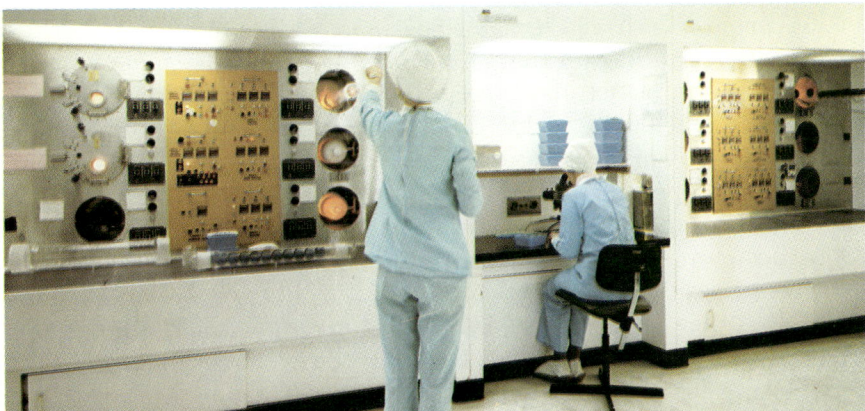

ABOVE LEFT A photo-lithography machine, being used here to produce very high density chips

ABOVE RIGHT A stack of wafers entering the oven

CENTRE Like some subminiature bakery, rows of ovens line the walls of this clean room where silicon chips are doped

BELOW Pure gold wire, thinner than a human hair, is used to join the tiny silicon chip to the metal 'spider' which provides it with electrical connections to the outside world

p-type doping, insulating layers may be produced by exposing the silicon to oxygen, metal connecting regions can be formed by vacuum deposition of aluminium and vertical structure can be created by etching the exposed areas with an acid. The completed chip may go through twenty such processing steps.

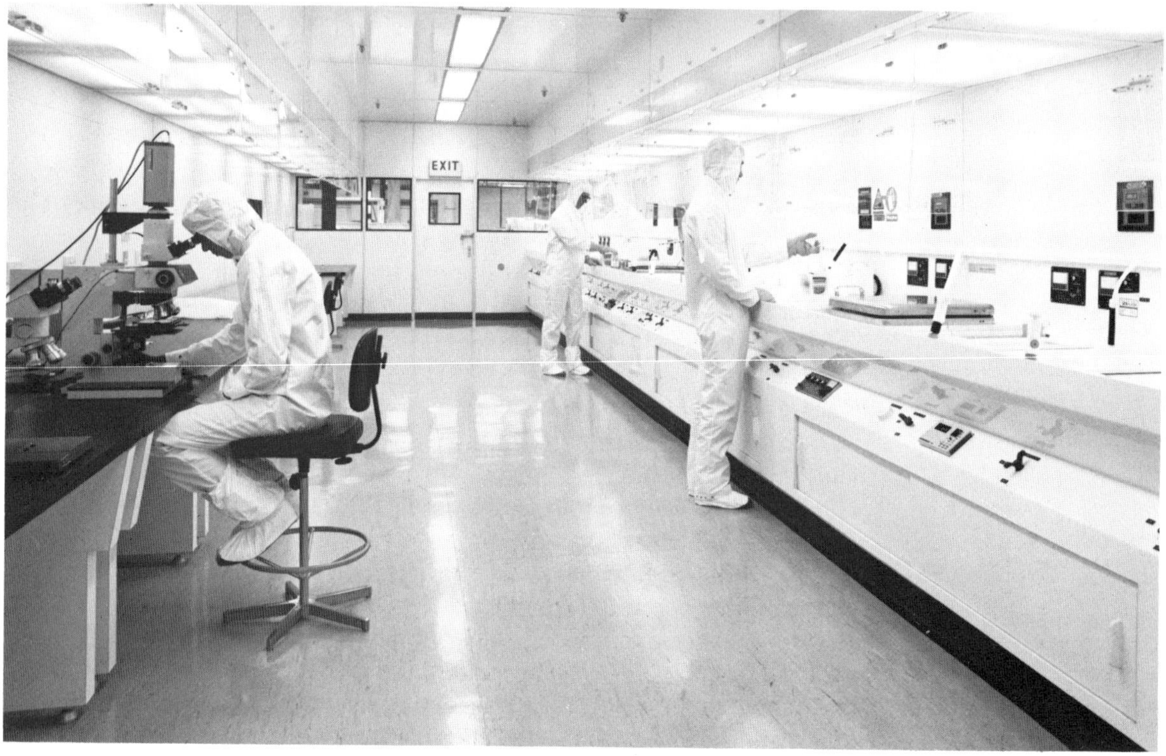

Integrated circuit photolithography is a superbly developed technology, but the problem it keeps running up against is that you cannot draw a fine line with a blunt pencil. At present it is producing doping regions as little as two micrometers (thousandths of a millimeter) across. But as the demand grows for dimensions of one micrometer and below so it is becoming necessary to look for techniques with a sharper point. The limiting factor is not, as we might expect, the quality of the cameras and films, nor the properties of the photo-resists, but the nature of light.

Visible light, the light we actually see, is just a tiny part of the spectrum of electromagnetic radiation, which also includes radio waves, infra-red, ultra-violet, X-rays and gamma rays. The only difference between these various forms of radiation is in their wavelengths. Radio waves have the greatest wavelengths, X-rays and gamma rays the shortest. Visible light fits in between infra-red and ultra-violet and covers the range from about 0.4 to 0.7 of a micrometer. That is, it has a wavelength of around half a micrometer. Now, it is a fundamental fact of physics that you can shine light through a hole provided that it is reasonably larger than the wavelength of your light. If it is smaller then no light will get through; if it is round about the same size then the light will be diffracted, that is, bent into complex patterns during its passage through the hole.

Cleanliness that would be the envy of any operating theatre is essential for all stages of chip manufacture

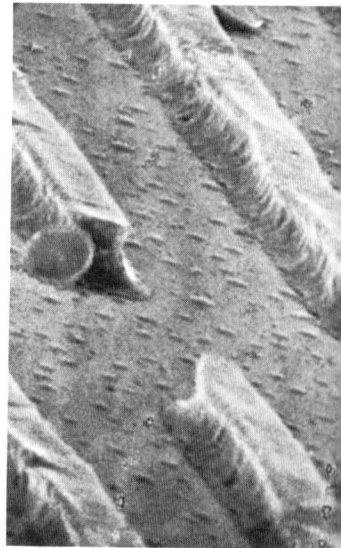

What it all comes down to is that two micrometers is about the smallest dimension you can hope to create with light. Try to draw anything smaller and you will find that the pencil is too blunt. The obvious solution, of course, is to use radiation of a shorter wavelength, and this indeed is how the industry is developing. But there is more to it than simply putting in a different type of light bulb. Visible light is easy to produce and relatively easy to control with glass optics but ultra-violet and, more especially, X-rays need entirely different techniques. What is more, a change in one part of the process immediately puts pressure on another part so that new types of mask and new resists also need to be developed.

The prospects for using ultra-violet are really quite good and scientists within the semiconductor industry are confident that the one-micrometer barrier will be broken very soon in regular production. But to reduce the size much further would require some very big changes.

X-rays have wavelengths below about 10 nanometers (1 nanometer =1/1000 micrometer) so they offer ample scope for future miniaturization. Experimental X-ray lithography has already managed to reproduce patterns with a size of 17 nanometers, which is at least a hundred times smaller than conventional visible-light methods can ever achieve. It is, however, high technology on a grand scale. The quality and intensity of the beam need to be such that simple X-ray tubes of the sort used in medicine are quite unsuitable. The only effective way of doing it at present is to use a large synchrotron.

Inside a synchrotron, electrons or other charged particles travel round a large hollow ring. Electromagnets which encircle the ring provide a varying magnetic field to accelerate the particles and keep them within the orbit. As the speed begins to approach that of light so the particles radiate energy, including X-rays, at a tangent to the circle. This radiation can be collected at so-called ports around the ring and used for whatever it is needed. Many experiments have already been done using machines like the Synchrotron Radiation Source at Daresbury Laboratory in England and a synchrotron at Brookhaven National Laboratory in New York. It is clear from these that X-ray lithography could become a very valuable technique for chip manufacture if the cost of providing synchrotron radiation ever fell low enough.

So far, only a few manufacturers have invested money in researching X-ray techniques and it does not seem that they will become part of the regular production process for some time to come. If they do then they will require some further development in the field of mask design, because as the patterns become finer so the masking layer needs to become thinner if it is to continue projecting a clean-edged image. Making thin X-ray masks is not too difficult: one possibility is a gold-coated sheet of plastic with the pattern etched out of the metal. The problem is how to keep a very thin mask absolutely flat without stretching or otherwise distorting the pattern.

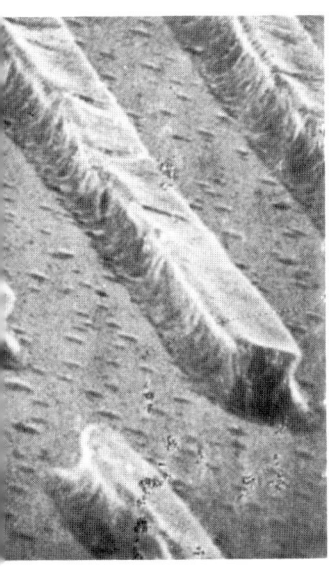

Seen with the electron microscope, this is part of a test pattern produced by X-ray lithography at the Daresbury Laboratory in Cheshire

X-ray lithography equipment at the Brookhaven Laboratory in New York State. A silicon wafer is just being mounted in the end of the X-ray beam line

The problem may never arise, however, because other lines of research are opening up new ways of printing patterns onto the resist without using a mask at all. Even more intriguing are new techniques that do away with the resist as well, allowing circuits to be 'painted' directly onto the silicon.

Video chips

In the world of entertainment, video technology is rapidly taking over from the traditional techniques of film and photography. Where, at one time, home movies flickered on a wobbly screen, now video games and laser disks glow on the phosphor screen. In place of the album filled with wedding photographs and holiday snaps there now stands a row of video cassettes. Much the same sort of change is starting to take place within the silicon factories where chips are made.

The fundamental limitations of using light, and the practical problems in using other types of electromagnetic radiation, have encouraged the scientists to look for new ways of putting patterns onto silicon. One of the most promising ideas has been to replace the photographic system with the same technique that makes our television screens come to life – beams of electrons.

Within the cathode-ray tube of a typical television set, a narrow beam of electrons is accelerated towards a phosphor screen; wherever it strikes the screen it produces a glow, whose brightness depends on the intensity of the beam at that point. In order to build up a complete picture, the electron beam is scanned across the screen in 625 horizontal lines, and to make the pictures move, the whole screen is rescanned 25 times every second. Because electrons have virtually no mass, the beam can be manoeuvred at great speed through such a complex pattern without ever overshooting on the corners or at the ends of lines. It is an impressive combination of speed and accuracy and it forms the basis not only of television sets, but also of scientific instruments such as electron microscopes and, more recently, of a chip-making technique called electron-beam lithography.

As the name suggests, this is similar to the more conventional photo-lithography in that the pattern for each layer is printed onto the resist, which then protects part of the surface during doping, etching, etc. The big difference is that there is no mask, instead the wafer, enclosed within a vacuum chamber, becomes the screen for a beam of electrons. The resist, no longer a photo-resist but one that is sensitive to the electron bombardment, has the pattern drawn directly onto it in all its intricate detail.

In principle it should be possible to get down to astonishingly fine dimensions, limited only by the size of individual molecules in the resist. In practice things are rather more complicated. Any electron entering the protective layer will tend to be deflected from its original path by the resist molecules, with the result that the beam as a whole becomes more diffuse. Electrons that get through to the silicon may also back-scatter, spreading the effects of the beam still further. The result is that what should have been a precise, narrow strip of hardened resist becomes a broader, fuzzy-edged band.

There seems to be little hope of preventing electron scatter, but help may come from a rather obscure invention dating back fifty years: the Langmuir–Blodgett film. Irving Langmuir was the man who invented the modern coiled filament, which has been used in light bulbs ever since. It was an invention of such vast commercial value that his employers, General Electric, gave him a laboratory and allowed him to pursue whatever research he wanted to for the rest of his career. Working with him in the laboratory was Kathleen Blodgett, a very successful chemist. Together, they devised a means of producing chemical layers precisely one molecule thick. It was an impressive achievement but they were unable to think of any practical use for it and so it lay in obscurity for many years. Today, Langmuir–Blodgett films have found their application – in making resists thin enough to be unaffected by electron scatter.

The basic idea behind the Langmuir–Blodgett film is the same as that which allows washing-up liquids to make the remains of greasy food soluble in water. Detergent molecules are more or less long and thin. One end, described as hydrophilic, can easily dissolve in water, the other end, called hydrophobic, is repelled by water but will attach itself readily to any non-watery object such as a lump of grease. The grease immediately becomes covered in a layer of molecules with water-attracting ends exposed and the overall piece, now made water soluble, floats off with little difficulty.

It is possible to make many different substances with this combination of hydrophilic and hydrophobic ends. If any such chemical is put into water it will form a surface layer with all the hydrophobic ends uppermost. By very smooth and gentle movement it is then possible to transfer this layer onto something like a sheet of glass or a wafer of silicon where it forms a Langmuir–Blodgett film one molecule deep. Repeatedly raising and lowering the material into the water produces a Langmuir–Blodgett multilayer with an exact number of molecules in its thickness.

In order to make an effective Langmuir–Blodgett resist, any material would have to be set solid by an electron beam, be totally resistant to all the etching and doping chemicals and, of course, have the necessary structure of hydrophilic and hydrophobic ends. It is a demanding list of specifications, but some suitable materials have already been found and the results are very encouraging. Several sets of experiments have produced lines one twentieth of a micrometre wide, which is a very respectable beginning for a new technology.

It would be rash to try to predict which of these techniques – uV, X-rays or electron beams – will dominate in the coming years. Whichever it is, it will not have a monopoly because there are many specialized processes that are needed for particular applications. Lasers, for example, are used to produce very localized changes in crystal structure and composition in order to make some types of chip. There is also a very promising technique called ion-beam lithography which uses high energy beams of electrically charged atomic nuclei to etch and dope silicon wafers directly. Techniques like these will all be important in the race to make even smaller computer circuits. But it is not the only race that must be run.

The successful development of computer circuitry depends on chips becoming both cheaper and faster. Reducing the size satisfies both these aims – small chips use less silicon and so cost less, and they are also faster because the signals do not have so far to travel within them. But speed is probably the more important criterion: we could accept an increase in cost if it led to better performance but would not accept a backward step to more primitive computers just because they were cheaper. Now, if making chips faster by making them smaller is proving difficult, why not make them faster by making them faster? The idea is not as eccentric as it appears.

An electric current is a passage of electrons through a substance and so its speed will depend directly on how fast electrons are able to move in that material. Altering the material or the conditions under which it operates may allow faster electron movement and hence faster computers. This sort of change has already happened once: in the early days of semiconductor electronics, long before silicon chips came along, transistors were all made from germanium, a material that was very difficult to obtain, too sensitive to temperature, and did not allow electrons to flow through it very fast. The move to silicon alleviated all three problems in one easy step. Perhaps we could now find a super-semiconductor that will work even faster.

Computing at absolute zero

In the late 1960s a British engineer, Brian Josephson, predicted mathematically that a strange thing should happen at temperatures near to absolute zero. His work was too complex to attract much general attention but several laboratories became very interested and decided to take a look. They found that Brian Josephson was right, a strange thing was indeed happening and it created a new type of computer circuit. The Josephson junction which resulted from this research is a computer

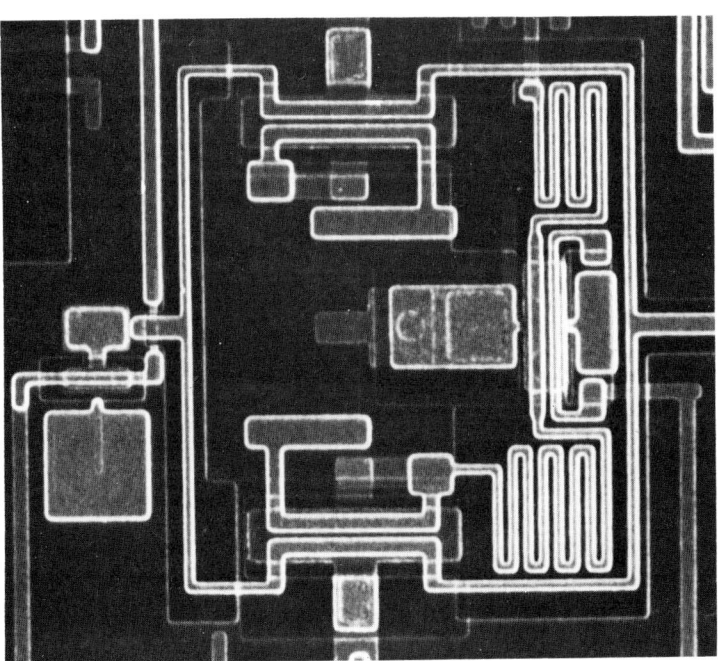

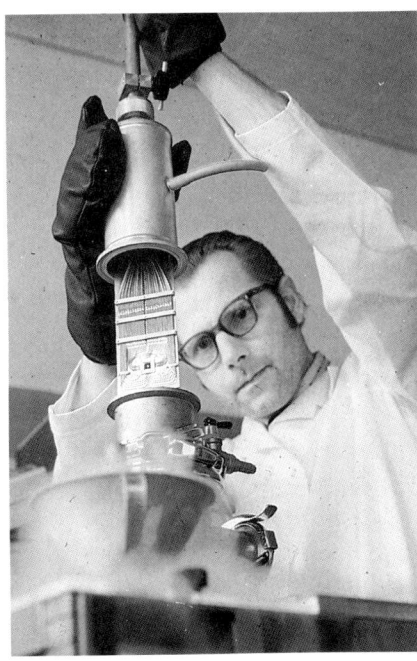

LEFT A Josephson junction circuit greatly magnified. The junction itself is the small circle in the center of the picture

RIGHT An IBM researcher at the Zurich research laboratory lowering a Josephson device into liquid helium in preparation for a Josephson experiment

memory device at least ten times faster than the best conventional electronics. Its operation depends on two extraordinary effects, both of which had been known about for some time. The first is superconductivity, the second is called tunnelling.

At normal temperatures all electrical conductors, even the very best, offer some resistance to the flow of electric current. The effect is to convert the energy within the current into heat - we see this every day in the heating up of an electric fire or a light bulb. But if the temperature is taken down close to absolute zero ($-273.16°C$) then some conductors will suddenly lose all their resistance and become superconductors. An electric current could flow virtually for ever round a ring of superconducting material without needing any sort of power input to keep it going, and without producing any heating effect whatsoever.

Tunnelling is, if anything, even more bizarre. It rests on one of the most powerful and fundamental of scientific theories: quantum mechanics, which strives to explain the nature of matter at its most basic level. It is a prediction of this theory that an electron can cross an extremely thin barrier without in any sense having gone through it. In effect, it disappears on one side of the barrier and instantly reappears on the other.

Tunnelling occurs at any temperature and it is utilized in a number of specialized electronic devices, but Josephson's prediction was that it could be combined with superconductivity in a particularly useful way. He proposed that a loop of superconducting material should be broken by an extremely thin layer of insulator. Under normal conditions a current could flow indefinitely around the loop, tunnelling its way through the insulating barrier on every orbit. The result would be that a small voltage could be measured across the barrier. However, if a strong enough magnetic field were applied to the device, the superconductivity would be destroyed and the voltage across the barrier would change.

In this rather complex way, the Josephson junction can be used to store a single bit of computer information. Because there is no intermediate position – either the current flows round the loop or not – it fits in perfectly with the needs of a binary system dealing with 1s and 0s. Its big advantage compared to conventional memory circuits is that pulses may be stored and retrieved extremely quickly (it takes around ten trillionths of a second). In addition, because the whole thing works with superconduction, there is no heat generated by the flow of electricity and so the individual memory cells can be packed very tightly together with no risk of overheating.

A good deal of money and research effort has gone into perfecting the Josephson junction computer and the results are very impressive, if not yet entirely practical. Maintaining the very low temperature is relatively easy using liquid helium, which can keep the junctions at just 4° above absolute zero. The problem is that once it is immersed within the liquid helium, the computer becomes quite inaccessible. If anything needs maintenance or modification the whole assembly has to be very slowly and carefully brought back up to room temperature so as to avoid damaging the delicate Josephson junctions.

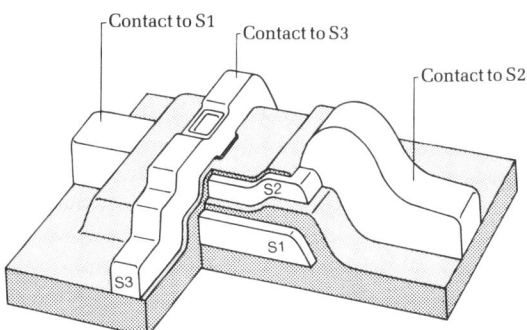

The quiteron, like the Josephson junction, operates at temperatures near to absolute zero. The three regions S1, S2 and S3 are made of a superconducting material, the shaded regions which separate them are insulating layers. By varying the voltage of S2 the device can be made to switch on or off in less than a third of a billionth of a second

An even bigger problem is in making the devices. The insulating barriers need to be so thin that a hundred thousand of them could be stacked side by side across a pinhead. Technology on that sort of scale does not come cheap, nor is it very reliable. Even so, Josephson junctions are the fastest computer circuits that have ever been made, although they only exist in research laboratories so far. But whether they become the standard technology for the hyper-fast computers of the future may well depend on the outcome of recent discoveries in another quite unrelated area: the superlattice.

The two-dimensional gas

When we talk of the speed of a semiconductor device we are referring to the time it takes to switch from one state to another – from 1 to 0 or from 0 to 1. Since an electric current is nothing more than a flow of electrons we are, in effect, considering how quickly that particular material allows the electrons to start moving and how fast their normal cruising speed will then be. Physicists measure these properties under the heading of electron mobility. Silicon has a higher mobility than germanium so it resulted in faster computer circuits. Perhaps other materials with an even higher mobility could offer the prospect of the very fast chips we are looking for.

The most promising candidate so far is a material called gallium arsenide. Unlike silicon and germanium, both of which are elements (substances that cannot be broken down chemically) gallium arsenide is a compound made up of the two elements gallium and arsenic. Its electron mobility is around thirty times higher than silicon's, giving it a speed advantage of about five times. Gallium arsenide devices have already established an important role in telecommunications electronics, particularly microwave equipment and satellite receivers, but they have yet to make a major impact on computing.

The main problem is in producing the fine detail needed for integrated circuits. In the case of silicon or germanium it is very easy to diffuse dopant impurities into the crystal structure. It is much harder to do so with gallium arsenide and so the conventional lithography techniques cannot readily be used. Until recently it looked as if gallium arsenide may have been just another of the unfulfilled promises of science, yet today its future looks very bright indeed. Two things happened: a piece of exotic physics research suggested a way of making gallium arsenide chips even faster, and a breakthrough in manufacturing technology offered the means of doing it.

In 1969 two scientists, Leo Esaki and Raphael Tsu, proposed the superlattice. Esaki was the man who had first suggested how to make use of the tunnelling effect in a semiconductor – work that had gained him a Nobel Prize for Physics. In the superlattice he proposed a sandwich structure made up of alternate layers of different semiconductors. If the layers were made thin enough, about a millionth of a centimeter, the crystal block as a whole should begin to exhibit strongly directional properties.

At right angles to the structure, electrons would tunnel their way through alternate layers giving the substance a bizarre property called negative conductivity. Normally, electricity follows the law that increasing the voltage increases the strength of the current. This is why a new battery gives a brighter flashlight beam than a used one. With negative conductivity the situation is reversed so that, within certain limits, increasing the voltage lowers the current and vice versa.

As if that were not strange enough, an even more peculiar thing happens to electrons moving along the layers: their mobility goes up hundreds, even thousands, of times. Within any ordinary semiconductor the electrons move like balls on a pinball machine, constantly being scattered and deflected by the fixed atoms of the crystal lattice. This obstacle course is what limits their mobility. In the superlattice it is almost as if the crystal had completely vanished and the current flows like gas through a pipe.

It took nine years before anyone managed to produce a superlattice to test the predictions. They turned out to be true: along the layers, thin sheets of current flowed like a two-dimensional gas.

A great deal of work still has to be done before this laboratory curiosity becomes an everyday component of our computers. But it seems likely that extremely fast devices could be produced in this way. The very high mobility provides speed while the tunnelling effect at right angles provides a way of switching the current on and off. Keeping the chips cold speeds them up even further, without the need for going as low as absolute zero.

Devices that make use of the superlattice are described as 'modulation doped' because the level of doping goes up and down as we cross successive layers. The main research effort up to now has concentrated

OPPOSITE Part of a molecular beam epitaxy machine. Sprouting from around the main vacuum chamber are molecular beam guns, viewing ports, manipulators and a cryogenic pump. A machine like this can process up to 60 wafers per hour and position its doping regions with an accuracy of 0.05 micron

Electrons in a semiconductor are bounced from atom to atom like balls on a pinball machine. The less obstructed their path, the faster they can travel

on using layers of pure gallium arsenide alternating with layers of aluminium–gallium arsenide that has been doped with silicon atoms to make it n-type. There are various other combinations with tongue-twisting names like indium–aluminium arsenide and indium–gallium arsenide that are being tried.

Leo Esaki continues to produce theoretical predictions of how things could be speeded up even further. His latest proposal is for a polytype superlattice using three different materials in a repeating triple pattern. He suggests that compounds such as aluminium antimonide, gallium antimonide and indium arsenide could produce a polytype material without any need for doping. This would result in even greater mobility and might reduce manufacturing costs at the same time.

But all of these ideas would just be pie in the sky if it were not for the invention of a technique called molecular beam epitaxy (MBE). All of the compound semiconductors, like gallium arsenide, make it difficult for dopant atoms to work their way into the crystal structure. MBE offers a way of growing the crystal, one molecular layer at a time, and introducing the dopant as it grows. It not only gets around the doping problem but also produces the precisely thin layers needed for superlattice materials.

Starting with a small base crystal, or substrate, of pure gallium arsenide, the superlattice is built up by directing beams of the constituent molecules onto it and allowing them to condense on the surface. The beams are produced from small quantities of ultra-pure material (gallium, aluminium, silicon, arsenic, etc.) contained within heated cells which can vaporize them rapidly. The whole process has to be carried out under extreme vacuum and within a liquid nitrogen shroud which freezes out any remaining impurities in the vacuum chamber. By varying the temperature of each cell it is possible to control the density of its molecular beam, while mechanical shutters over the front of the cell switch the beam on and off. It provides an unparalleled means of accurately controlling the crystal structure.

In order to produce our superlattice of gallium arsenide alternating with n-type aluminium-gallium arsenide, a simple rhythmic pattern is followed. The gallium and arsenic shutters remain permanently open because they are needed for both materials, while the aluminium and silicon ones open and shut simultaneously to produce the interleaved layers. Changing over the raw materials allows us just as easily to produce any of the other compound semiconductors, with or without doping.

By now it may seem that with so many wonderful breakthroughs the future of very fast and very small chips is safely assured. Well, in a way it is, because there are now enough options available and there is more than enough incentive for producing them. But it would be wrong to suggest that the way ahead is clearly visible. The computer industry depends on a high degree of standardization at the chip level in order to

Chip factory of the future. Replacing rooms full of ovens, baths and so on, this one machine manufactures and tests gallium arsenide semiconductors. It can take ten wafers in one loading

allow mass production and low unit costs. It is going to take commercial wrangling as well as scientific research to determine whether the future standard will be Josephson junctions, modulation-doped superlattices or something altogether more prosaic.

However, three things seem clear about the technology of tomorrow's world. Firstly, that whichever approach is chosen, very high speed computers will have to be refrigerated in order to squeeze out the maximum switching speeds. Secondly, that there will always be a need for highly specialized techniques and materials to cope with some applications. Thirdly, that for less demanding tasks, silicon processed by electron beams or X-rays will remain the material of choice because of its low cost and ease of handling.

But what happens in the day-after-tomorrow's world? The seeds of technological change are often sown long before any new applications can be harvested and today crystals are not the only things being grown in computer labs.

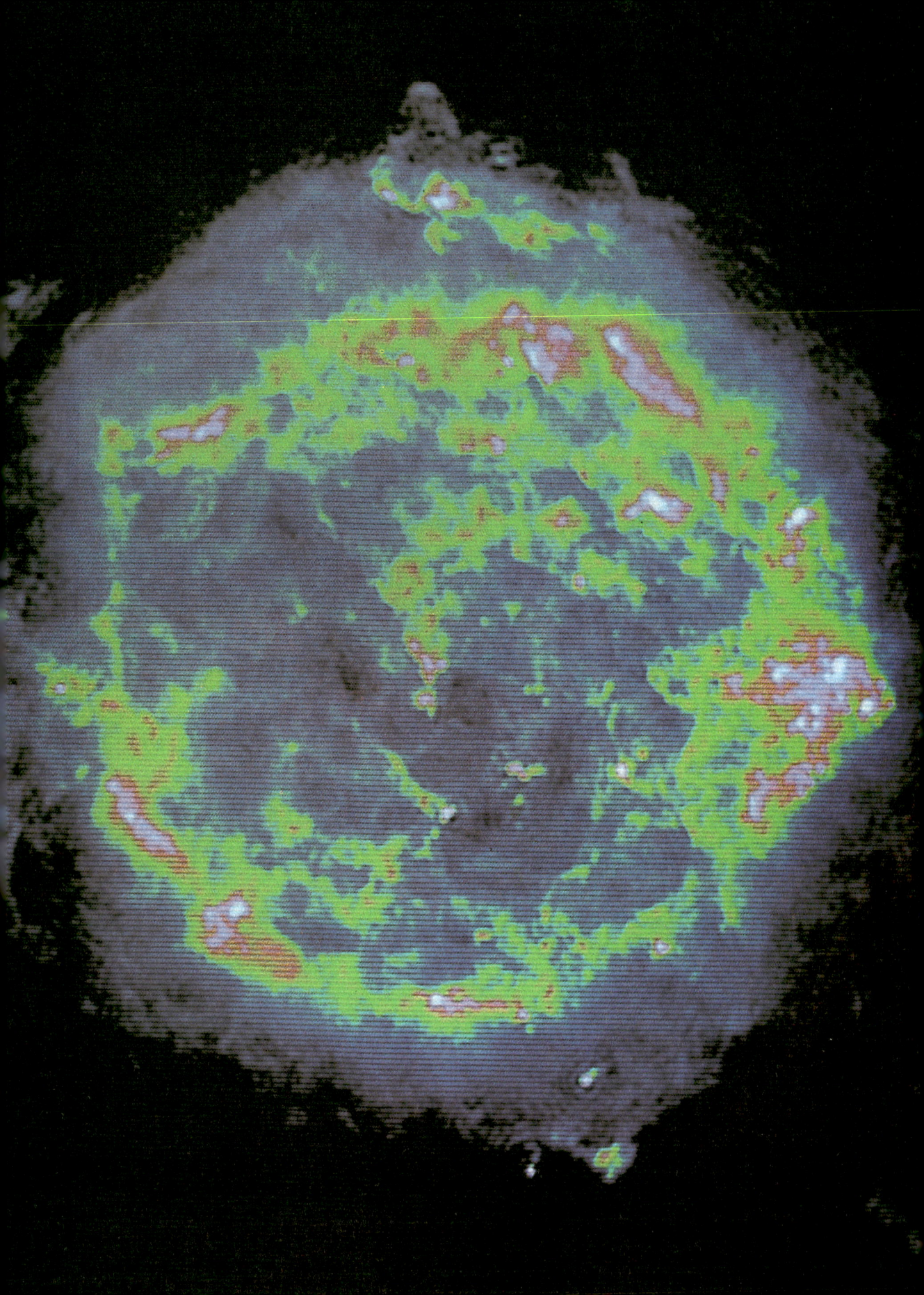

CHAPTER SEVEN
Beyond the Silicon Chip

Around five and a half billion (thousand million) years ago, in a dusty outer corner of our galaxy, a star exploded as a supernova. The violence of the event was such that individual atoms of starstuff were ripped apart and reassembled into new elements. At the same time, a thunderous shock wave of expanding matter was hurled out, mixing and compressing the scattered cloud of dust and gas already present in this region of space.

The jolt was sufficient to start the cloud collapsing inwards under its own gravitational pull, a process that led to the formation of our sun (and probably several other stars which have since drifted away). Around the developing sun there remained a rotating disk of dust, gas and rocky debris, which soon began its own process of compaction; larger pieces swept up smaller ones in a spiralling growth which created the planets.

Energy released by the decay of radioactive materials, the squeezing together of the center and the continuous bombardment of additional particles was sufficient to melt the young Earth. As it melted, so the denser material sank towards the core while lighter substances floated up to the surface. By around four billion years ago enough heat had been lost for the outer crust to begin solidifying and the broad pattern of internal layers was established. The process of segregation, in which denser material, especially iron, sank inwards to form the core, brought to the surface lighter minerals based primarily on silicon and aluminium. As a result, 60 per cent of the Earth's crust is now made up of the substance silica – the raw material from which pure silicon is obtained for use in chips.

Even after the crustal rocks had cooled, the Earth was an alien and inhospitable planet with little oxygen in the atmosphere and little water on the surface. Yet less than a billion years later, the first known living organisms were forming colonies in shallow lakes and seas. The special chemistry that made possible that transition from non-life to life and which lies behind the subsequent evolution of all living systems could, according to some scientists, provide a basis for future computers which go far beyond silicon.

The growing computer

This is not a Frankenstein tale of artificially created life nor is it concerned with the suggestion, raised by some people, that computers are in any case emerging as a new and different type of life form. The question being asked is not 'Are computers alive?', but rather 'Does life compute?'. If it does, then some of its techniques may usefully be applied to the design of computing machines.

Suppose that you take a jigsaw puzzle, put all the pieces into a large box and shake them about. What chance is there that they will spontaneously fall together into a perfectly formed picture? It is probably as unlikely as the proverbial monkey at a typewriter producing the

ABOVE Stromatolites – fossilised mats of algae which were probably some of the earliest living organisms on earth

OPPOSITE The most recent supernova in our region of the galaxy is called Cassiopeia-A; it appeared about 325 years ago. In this radio telescope image, the expanding shell of matter is clearly visible, surrounded by the shock wave which appears as the blue outer ring

complete works of Shakespeare. And yet similar tasks can easily be done, indeed are being done all the time.

Inside our bodies many of the most important jobs are carried out by large protein molecules. The antibodies that help to protect us against infection, the hemoglobin that carries oxygen in the blood stream, the enzymes that digest our food and many more vital chemicals are all protein molecules. Many proteins have an extremely complex three-dimensional shape which gives them their special properties. The largest of them contain tens of thousands of individual atoms made up into sub-units which join together to form the complete molecule.

It is relatively easy to break down a protein into its sub-units but even simpler to build it up again. Shake the pieces together and the three-dimensional jigsaw will spontaneously reassemble into a perfectly formed protein. The process requires no special treatment and it will even happen in a jumbled mixture of many different proteins. But in the 1960s scientists made an even more remarkable discovery. They were able to obtain all the constituent parts of a virus called Bacteriophage T4; they mixed them together in a test tube and found that perfect T4 viruses had been spontaneously produced.

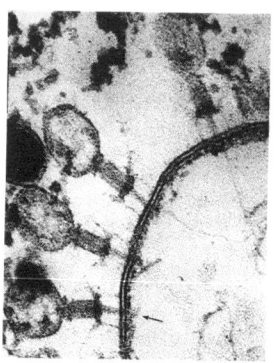

T4 viruses attached by their piercing ends to a bacterium

It was a significant observation because the bacteriophage is a complex and very precise structure. It is shaped rather like a tadpole with a hexagonal 'head' at one end and a hollow tube for the tail. The tube is used like a syringe in order to pierce the outer wall of a bacterium into which the virus then injects its own DNA. The DNA fools the bacterium into producing more viruses which build up inside it. Eventually, unable to contain the load, it bursts, releasing them to infect other bacteria. In experiments the test-tube bacteriophages performed this job perfectly.

The fact that very complex molecular structures are able to assemble themselves in this way has been an important finding for scientists who are trying to understand how the first simple life forms came together. It is also of significance to computer scientists because a virus like Bacteriophage T4 is about one tenth of a micrometer in length: in other words one tenth the size now being achieved with masks and photo-resists. It will not take many more years before chip manufacture gets down to the dimensions of a large protein molecule. When it does, we shall be doing the hard way what nature can do so easily: build very fine and very precise structures. Could we not learn a lesson from nature then and make it build our computers for us?

Science fiction? Not at all. Molecular computers have not been produced yet, but the research is being taken very seriously indeed. Britain's Science and Engineering Research Council has set up a special Molecular Electronics Panel to guide this type of study and there is considerable interest within the universities. In the United States and Japan, too, research projects have now been started specifically to develop and exploit the technology.

Natural crystals, like these amethysts, owe their shapes to the regular arrangement of their atoms. In that sense they are very simple

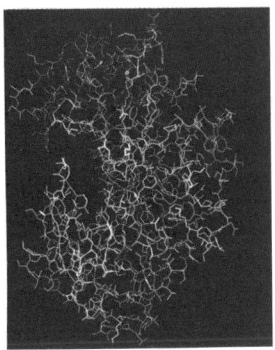

Proteins are much more complex and irregular

What began as a uniform wafer of pure silicon has had over a hundred intricate chips fabricated onto it. Molecular electronics offers the prospect of achieving this same sort of complexity but built up from the bottom

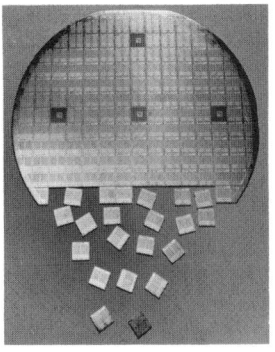

There are three good reasons for this activity. Firstly, size: a truly three-dimensional molecular computer will have, it is estimated, one billion times the capacity of a silicon computer of the same size. Secondly, cost: the technologies required for manufacturing conventional chips will become even more expensive as size is reduced. By contrast, producing molecular components may require less sophisticated equipment while offering the same advantages of mass production. Thirdly, speed: molecular computers offer the prospect of parallel processing on a scale never before imagined. For some tasks, like computer vision, this may be the only way to go.

Ultimately the aim would be to produce a protein computer that would self-assemble out of units manufactured by genetically engineered bacteria. But long before that becomes a reality the ideas embodied in molecular electronics are likely to bring other important developments. Molecular layers are already being deposited onto ordinary semiconductors in order to modify their properties. There is also a good deal of commercial as well as academic interest in producing organic semiconductors – materials which are chemically similar to plastics but have the electrical properties of a semiconductor.

The common factor in all these areas of development is the use of molecular rather than crystalline structures. Silicon, as it is used for chips, is a crystal just like diamond or salt. In other words it is a regularly repeating pattern of atoms; provided that there are no defects present, any one part of the crystal should look like any other. Because of this regularity crystals can be grown quite easily, each additional layer lining up with those already present. In this sense crystals self-assemble just like proteins do. The difference is that crystals are essentially very simple, like a regular wallpaper pattern, whereas proteins are extremely complex and irregular.

When a chip designer begins the task of converting a small sliver of silicon into a functional computer circuit he starts, in effect, with a blank sheet of paper. Pure silicon stretches in every direction waiting for the required complexity to be fabricated into it. Molecular electronics approaches this task from the opposite end; instead of working down to the required detail it builds it up from the bottom.

Of course, it is one thing to marvel at the way that protein molecules can arrange themselves into very complicated and precise shapes; but quite another to make use of that complexity in a computing circuit. What makes scientists believe that a lump of protein, however intricate, could do arithmetic or word processing or cartoon animation?

The plastic computer
Chemistry divides into two broad areas called inorganic and organic. Substances such as salt, baking powder, rust or bleach are all inorganic. Plastics, sugar, petrol and proteins are organic; the name does not mean that these things necessarily came from living organisms, although it is

true that almost all the chemistry of life is organic. The factor that they have in common is that they are based on the element carbon.

The particular way in which carbon atoms are able to make chemical bonds with each other or with different atoms gives organic chemistry the ability to form large and complex molecules. Rings, long chains, branched tree shapes, tangled balls and twisted coils are all there. The beautiful double helix of DNA which encodes the master plans for all of life is in this category. So are the very long thin molecules, tangled like a plate of spaghetti, that slip past each other to give rubber its stretch and bounce. At the other extreme is a molecule like hemoglobin which one biologist has described as looking like a thornbush, so dense is its architecture.

This intricacy, rather than being an unwanted complication, is believed by many to be the very key to creating the self-assembling molecular computer and, eventually, a biological computer. But even the humblest of these large organic molecules have something to offer.

What you and I call plastics the organic chemists call polymers. A polymer is a long chain molecule made up of many simple building blocks called mers. The shortest length possible is a single monomer, while the longest polymer may contain millions of mers. The properties of these materials come from the structure of the basic units and from the way they are joined together. The length of an individual molecule is unimportant and any piece of plastic will contain a great variety of long and short molecules tangled and intertwined together.

Now, on the face of it, plastics may seem to be the very last area where we would look for new materials to replace silicon chips and copper wire. They are after all remarkably good insulators. Look at any electrical lead around the house and the chances are that it will be covered with a protective layer of plastic insulation. Yet scientists had felt for many years that it ought to be possible to create plastics that would conduct electricity. A few of these have now been produced and found to offer some intriguing properties that go beyond the ordinary notion of conductors and semiconductors.

The simplest and potentially most interesting of these is a plastic called polyacetylene. It consists of a zigzag backbone of carbon atoms to each of which is attached one hydrogen. We saw earlier that each type of atom has a characteristic number of outer electrons which form bonds to adjacent atoms. Carbon has four of these valence electrons and so can make four bonds. Hydrogen has only one. This leads to an interesting situation: each carbon in the polyacetylene chain is joined to one carbon on its left, one on its right and to one hydrogen, which leaves one valence electron spare. If all these spare electrons remained unused then polyacetylene would certainly be an electrical conductor. What actually happens is that alternate pairs of carbon atoms form a double bond, satisfying the needs of all their valence electrons and keeping to the tradition that polymers are insulators.

The Severn Bore – a solitary wave, or soliton, which can travel for miles up the River Severn. It is fast moving and very little affected by most obstacles in its path

For years polyacetylene languished in obscurity until researchers at the University of Pennsylvania began to investigate the use of impurities to affect the electrical properties of an organic substance. What happened next should sound very familiar: they found that doping polyacetylene with tiny amounts of a substance that could donate an electron, or one that could accept an electron into a hole, dramatically altered the material's conductivity. In fact, by suitable doping they could take polyacetylene through the whole range from insulator to semiconductor to conductor. Nobody is yet certain just how polyacetylene semiconductors work, but at least it is now established that polyacetylene can produce electronic devices.

If it were simply that it offered yet another semiconductor material, polyacetylene would not be all that interesting; but research has indicated a way in which it may become directly applicable to the development of a molecular computer. This makes use of what are called solitons. Imagine that you are travelling along the roller-coaster back of a polyacetylene chain. There are two possible patterns you could meet – either you would be going up a double bond and down a single or the other way round. But what happens if, half way through, the polymer flips over from one pattern to the other? You get a soliton.

A soliton is a rather complex mathematical idea, discovered by the British naval architect John Scott Russell on a canal in 1844. Riding along the towpath, Russell observed a barge whose bow wave continued to move ahead when the barge had stopped. For as long as he was able to gallop after it, the mysterious wave moved on without changing its shape or getting any weaker. Like that better-known example the Severn Bore, it was a soliton or solitary wave. Today the theory of solitons is used in designing special lasers and in helping to understand some problems of particle physics. It also explains the way that electricity may travel along a polyacetylene molecule.

At the point where the pattern of bonds flips over, the local electrical charge behaves like a soliton. Once a soliton is present in the backbone it can move in either direction along the polymer; all it takes is for one carbon bond to flip over to the other side at every step. Because the carbon atom that is at the soliton has only three bonds it also has one unused electron – so the passage of the soliton is also an electric current.

The zigzag backbone of carbon and hydrogen atoms which makes up a long molecule of polyacetylene. Where the pattern flips over the carbon atom has a spare electron – this soliton may move either way along the chain if one of the adjacent atoms flips its double bond to the other side

By joining three chains at a point, or by replacing some of the hydrogen atoms with more complex side chains, researchers have shown that it should be possible to produce plastic gates, switches and memory devices using solitons. In fact, with the addition of some suitably doped polymer to provide the connecting wires it should be possible to make the completely plastic computer.

It must be said that these ideas are still largely theoretical but they have a strong appeal, not least because one of the strange properties of a soliton is that none of its energy is ever lost as it travels along and so there is no heating effect. This is likely to be of major importance because the incredibly small and fragile devices of a molecular computer would burn to a cinder with conventional electric currents.

There are still many obstacles to producing a new plastic electronics. Polyacetylene, for example, is very unstable in air. What is more, all conducting polymers are very difficult to process – most of them do not melt, nor will they dissolve in any known liquid. Polyacetylene can be made as a thin film but most of the others are fine black powders which stubbornly refuse to join together. Where scientists have been successful in producing soluble versions the results tend to give very poor electrical performance.

A good deal of research is obviously still needed but there is no lack of interest in pursuing it. The prize would be a cheap, light, easy-to-produce material that offered all the functions of ordinary electronics but on a much smaller scale. If it could also be made to work without overheating then its future would look very good indeed.

Molecular metals

One of the more obvious contrasts between semiconducting polymers and conventional semiconductors is the vast difference between the

Long needle-like crystals of the molecular metal TMTSF$_2$PF$_6$

jumbled, tangled structure of one and the neat crystal patterns of the other. But organic chemistry has its crystals, too, and one group of these, called molecular metals, offers another distinct approach to computer circuitry.

With names like 7,7,8,8-tetracyano-p-quinodimethane, most molecular metals have, understandably, become known by more manageable initials like TCNQ and TMTSF. What they have in common is flat molecules which crystallize into neatly arranged stacks. Some of these materials behave like n-type semiconductors, others like p-type, and experiments suggest that combinations of molecular metals could provide very fast computer circuits. Like some of the polymers, they are able to make use of solitons and so avoid some of the problems of overheating.

The potential impact of even this very simple approach to molecular electronics (after all we have not yet reached anything like the complexity of a protein molecule) is enormous. Remember the one micrometre barrier which silicon photolithography is currently attacking? Well, one of the first molecular electronic devices to have been designed is a diode employing the molecular metals TCNQ and TTF. Its overall length is two thousandths of a micrometer. This is miniaturization with a vengeance.

The benefits of such a size reduction are clear enough but there are problems also. Once you have made these devices how do you connect them all together in the right combination to produce a computer? This was much easier in the days when each electronic component was a separate item with wires sticking out of it. You simply assembled the circuit using bits of wire to join everything together in the required pattern. Silicon chips are not so very different – the work is done by chemicals rather than with soldering irons, but the designer still has absolute control over the positioning of all the components and their interconnections. But how do you arrange and connect together a test tube full of electronic molecules?

There is a point in scientific progress when head scratching, pencil chewing and scribbling mathematical formulae on the backs of envelopes no longer provide the answers. This is a time when even the most respectable scientist may turn the VDU screen towards a corner and play computer games.

Gliders, blinkers and honey farms

One game they often play is the game of Life. It is one of the simplest computer games there is and yet one of the most subtle. It is played on a square grid, the larger the better, so that the game never reaches the edges. Each square on the grid can either be empty or may contain a cell. Starting from whatever arrangement of cells you choose to put in, the whole pattern moves forward a generation at a time. At each generation some cells die, others are born and some existing ones survive. What

112 TOMORROW'S WORLD: COMPUTERS

Patterns of Life

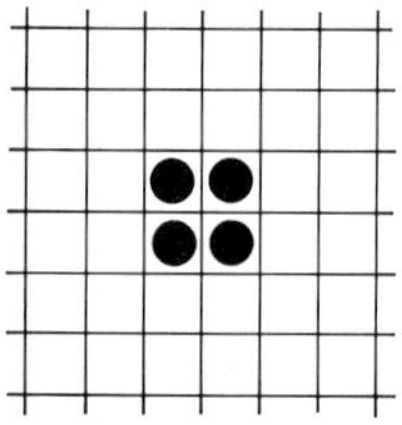

LEFT A square of four cells is stable and unchanging

RIGHT The 'blinker' alternates between the vertical and the horizontal

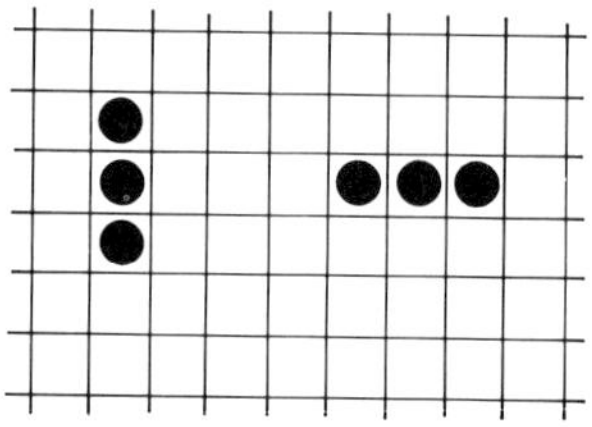

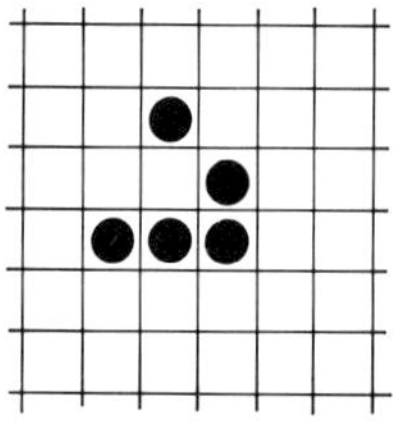

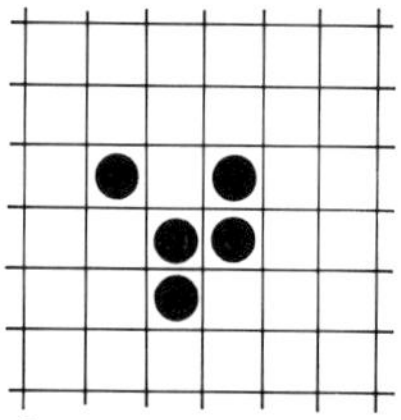

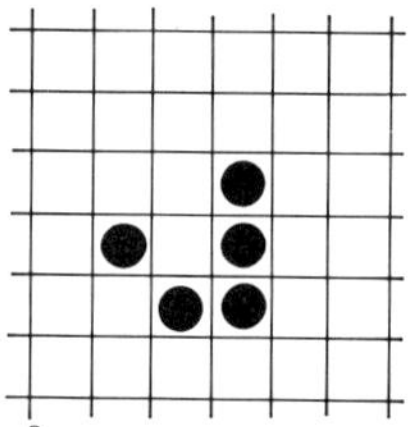

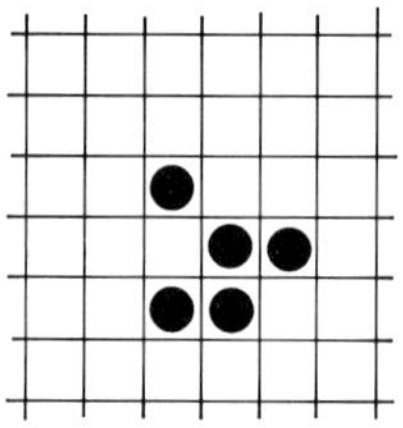

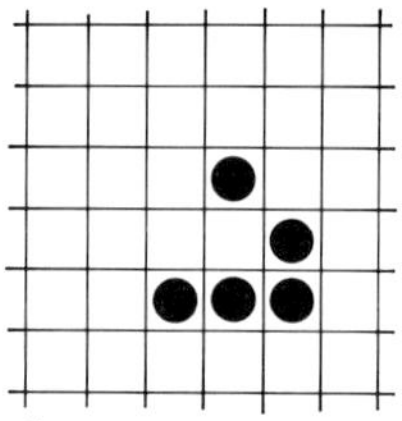

The glider moves diagonally one place after four generations (DIAGRAMS 1–5)

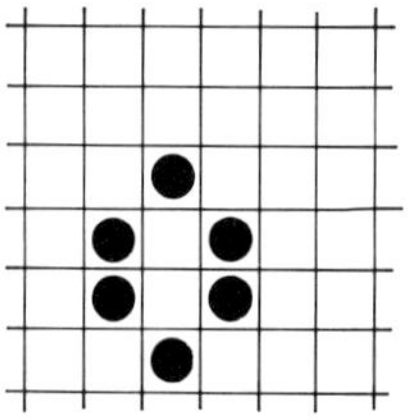

LEFT The 'beehive' is another stable shape. A cluster of 'beehives' makes a 'honey farm'

happens in any particular square depends on the state of the eight squares surrounding it. If a cell has less than two neighboring cells or more than three it dies. An empty square with exactly three adjacent cells has a new cell born in it. Cells with either two or three neighbors survive to the next generation.

The computing required to act out these simple rules is very straightforward and Life programs are readily available for even the smallest of home microcomputers. There is no opponent to play against, you just put in a starting pattern and follow its changing shape as it grows and decays. It seems no more useful than watching pretty patterns in a kaleidoscope, yet Life and its related games are bristling with analogies to physics, biology and mathematics. Some computer scientists, in particular, have found that they offer powerful new ideas for the future.

Life is a game with many levels. At the simplest we observe individual cells being born or dying – it is just a pattern of lights flashing on and off. But at the next level up we begin to notice certain very simple groups of cells that have their own properties. For example, a square made up of four adjoining cells is completely stable; left in isolation it will never change. A line of three cells is called a 'blinker' because it alternates between the horizontal and the vertical but otherwise never moves and never changes. A simple grouping of five cells makes a 'glider', which floats across the screen, moving one position in every four generations.

Adjust your mental eyes to a larger scale and you can see quite complex patterns grow, decay, fragment and give birth to new shapes. Intricate symmetrical patterns often blossom outwards very rapidly and then, just as suddenly, break up as overcrowding destroys their form. As cell colonies expand and contract they collide with other groups of cells and suddenly the whole development changes course. To experienced eyes the whole process can be observed on several different levels at once, all of them interacting but also, to a degree, independent of each other.

All good fun, but how does this relate to grand ideas about the future of computers? Well, the link is direct and rather surprising because the flowing, flickering patterns of Life are not only being produced by a computer, they actually *are* a computer – a type of computer that is very relevant to such problems as how to organize a molecular chip or how to produce robot vision.

Consider what computers do when they are working. They take in data, process it and produce an output. At a simple level the input may be a key being pressed on the keyboard and the output is the appearance of that letter on a screen. On a larger scale the input may be hundreds of readings from sensors in a power station which are processed together to result in many output signals controlling valves, conveyor belts, warning signals and so on. The same sort of thing happens in the patterns of Life.

Take the simplest level – the individual square. It has eight inputs coming from the surrounding squares, it processes them by adding them together and then produces an output in the form of cell or no-cell according to the result. Then it waits until it is time for the next calculation. Now move up to a higher level. The patterns that grow and swirl across the screen take in data of a more complex nature as they collide and interact with other patterns of cells. The results may not be as easy to predict but they still follow the rules of Life. What is needed is a way of using these patterns so that they perform useful computing.

There are various ways in which this could be done. For example, we could try to imitate the pulse sequences of the binary system using the five-cell glider to represent a pulse. By devising patterns that will either emit a pulse or not according to whether other glider pulses are present, we could develop something that works just like a gate circuit and employs the same rules which all electronic computers already use. Because gliders travel across the grid in straight lines, a vast layout of these patterns could send strings of pulses between each other just like electric pulses travelling along a wire.

Such a machine could certainly be made to work, but it would be ridiculously large and slow because it fails to make use of one of the most important properties of these pattern computers: since all the squares on the grid move forward simultaneously from one generation to the next this is the ultimate parallel architecture. There could be thousands, millions, or even more, simple computing elements all performing the same function in unison. What is needed is a way of using this power to best advantage.

It is an area where research is now making rapid progress. One of the first tasks was to examine the different sorts of rules that govern how one generation changes into the next. Many of these rules lead to completely trivial and predictable results, but there are also several with quite extraordinary properties. One example, even simpler than Life, uses the rule that, for every square on the grid, you count up the number of cells among its eight neighboring squares. If the number is odd then you put a cell into that square in the next generation; if it is even the square is made empty. This rule can take an initial pattern, reduce it rapidly to a quite disorganized-looking jumble then, suddenly, out of this mess produce eight perfect replicas of the original pattern.

Imagine what that could mean for the creation of a super-parallel computer. You feed in a pattern that represents, say, an image to be recognized. Using this rule, you very rapidly create eight copies of it. Then you change the rules in each of those eight areas to provide different types of processing. Not only are you analysing the image in eight ways at once but within each area all the squares are being processed in parallel.

Of course, there is a lot of work still to be done in finding the most appropriate rules and in creating computer circuits that allow useful data to be fed in and read out of these pattern grids. But already, scientists at the University of Warwick, for instance, are well advanced in developing VLSI (very large-scale integrated circuit) chips which will use these cellular patterns for jobs like image processing. In another year or two the results of their research are likely to be entering regular use. By the end of the century we can hope to see these pattern devices starting to have a profound effect on many areas of computing.

One of the great advantages of these pattern computers, particularly for image processing, is that information can be fed directly onto the grid by physically projecting the image onto the chip. All semiconductors are to a greater or lesser extent sensitive to light, which has a direct electrical effect on them, so this technique allows a complete image to be put into the circuit in one go – in parallel. As we have already seen, the pattern computer does its processing in parallel and when it comes to extracting the results, often all that is needed is to measure the density of cells in the final pattern to indicate whether or not a particular type of feature was present: a parallel process from start to finish.

Robot cloning

Life is just one example, perhaps the best known but not necessarily the most important, of what are called cellular automata. They were first suggested by Stanislaw Ulam, a Polish-born mathematician who worked on the development of the atom bomb in America, and were developed by his colleague John von Neumann, the same man who, five years earlier, had invented the stored-program computer. The essential characteristic of all cellular automata is that they consist of a regular layout of units each of which can exist in at least two different states. The whole layout steps forward one generation at a time, the state of every point being dependent in some way on its own and some or all of its neighbours' states in the previous generation.

In the case of Life or the pattern replicator we were dealing with a flat grid made up of squares, each of which could take on one of two states: cell or empty. But we do not need to restrict ourselves in this way; we could allow each square to have three separate states – empty, cell type one or cell type two – with correspondingly more complex rules about how the cells appear, change and die. In fact, we could opt for as many states as we wanted. Then again, we could use a hexagonal grid instead of a square one; we could even think about three-dimensional grids. There are infinitely many different types of cellular automaton and even the simple square grid offers thousands of different rules for governing the response of a square to its neighbors.

Von Neumann's original intention in studying these strange patterns was to answer the question whether or not it is possible to construct a machine that can reproduce itself. Many people had said that robots would only ever be able to make things that were simpler than themselves. In the same way many people still believe that computers can never become cleverer than we are because computers are made by humans and the human brain could never devise something cleverer than itself. Using his cellular automata, von Neumann was able to show that this is not so: self-replicating robots are possible, computers can be cleverer than we are, complexity can be created out of simplicity.

In particular, von Neumann showed that below a certain critical size any self-reproducing machine would inevitably produce smaller, simpler offspring at every generation and so eventually die out. But above that size, self-reproduction and even evolution become possible. In fact von Neumann's solution required a cellular automaton of around 200,000 squares with 29 different states. A veritable monster compared to the Life game – and all this simply to produce a changing pattern of dots which could create additional copies of itself! It seems a trivial achievement and yet it has shed light on some very interesting and important areas.

Despite the speculations of science fiction writers, it was not at all obvious that machines could reproduce or that a computer program could be written which would subsequently improve itself. In devising the notion of cellular automata, von Neumann provided a way of studying systems that undergo evolution: they may be mechanical machines, they may be living organisms or they may be computers. In each of these areas the idea has led to new insights and expectations. But that is not all: in the process he also showed that his self-

These robot arms are performing a simple inspection task. But would it be possible to build a robot so sophisticated that it could manufacture perfect replicas of itself out of the raw materials?

The chip being held by this caterpillar is made of silicon. Molecular electronics offers the prospect of chips made from the same sorts of materials as the caterpillar itself

reproducing pattern would be a Turing machine – a universal computer. Subsequently it has been shown that many simpler cellular automata, including Life, can produce all the features needed to carry out any kind of computing.

When von Neumann died in 1957, Claud Shannon, a pioneer in the field of computers and telecommunications, wrote of his automata studies: 'The areas which he opened for exploration will not be mapped in detail for many years.' Even now it is still too early to see the whole web of interconnections that is being revealed by these ideas, but there has been, in the early 1980s, a mushrooming growth in the study of cellular automata. Scientists who are searching for the origins of life, engineers concerned with designing space probes, mathematicians with an interest in thermodynamics and, especially, computer scientists have been probing and extending the topic with notable success.

It is unlikely that cellular automaton machines would ever totally replace ordinary computer technology but for certain applications, and in combination with more conventional techniques, they hold great promise. In addition to image processing, it is reasonable to expect that areas such as speech recognition and AI research will soon be able to make use of them. Eventually, however, the hope must be that general-purpose computers may be built along these lines. Already, some mathematicians and theorists of computer science are developing specific techniques and programming languages for use with these future machines. Others are looking at how to build them.

A blank sheet of paper

The simplest way to make a cellular automation is to take an ordinary computer, program it with the rules and then set up the patterns within it. Done like this, the cellular automaton computer has no physical existence of its own; it exists solely as a phantom made up of data within another machine. What we have in fact, is a computer simulator, imitating the machine comparable to a flight simulator imitating an aircraft's performance.

As a means of designing cellular automaton computers this is the obvious first stage, but it is hardly efficient as a working model because every step in the simulated machine requires many steps in the real one. How, then, should we set about building a physical machine that works directly with the cell patterns? The place to start is at the lowest level: the empty grid. What we have there is a vast array of identical elements each of which only has to do a very simple processing job. There is absolutely no structure nor any special arrangement built into it.

This is quite unlike a typical microprocessor with its extremely intricate and highly specialized structure. On the other hand, does it not seem ready-made for the molecular computer? There we have a mass of identical molecular devices and no easy way of linking them together into any meaningful arrangement. The very thing that made molecular electronics difficult now becomes a positive virtue. Instead of struggling to fabricate complexity we leave the hardware as a uniform featureless surface, a blank sheet of paper if you like, and put all the intricacy into the electrical patterns written onto it. Ultimately, there may be no specialized devices for computer processing, just high-density arrays of simple elements which could have any required computing pattern loaded into them.

Of course, it is not quite as easy as that; we cannot use just any uniform surface, it has to be one that has within it the ability to build up and manipulate patterns according to some useful set of rules. This means that whatever simple units it is made of must be able to exist in at least two distinct and stable states. There must also be some way in which each unit can detect the present state of its neighbors and be influenced by them. It is a demanding specification and yet one that is peculiarly well suited to what molecular electronics has to offer.

We could, for example, use a molecular metal, the regular, stacked structure of its crystals producing a uniform grid. Each molecule within this array becomes one unit of the cellular automaton, with small changes of orientation or electrical charge being used to represent the different states.

But even more intriguing is the prospect of using proteins as the material of computing.

Enzymes (one group of proteins) attach themselves to other specific molecules by a combination of shape fit and an interaction of electrical charges. In the same way the electronic molecules, if tailored to fit snugly together, would respond to the distribution of electrical charge around them. This information from their surroundings could switch the molecules from one state to another, which in turn could affect that molecule's neighbors. Many natural proteins already have this ability to switch between states, often by means of a slight deformation of part of the intricate protein shape.

Nobody has made computing proteins yet; nobody even knows what they should look like. But the idea of putting cellular automaton computers on a uniform flat array of self-assembled protein molecules is certainly not all that far-fetched. Several commercial and academic laboratories are investigating the possibilities of this technique and if they can get it to work its impact will be tremendous. Eventually, it may allow us to use nature to build our computers for us.

Bits from bugs
One of the fastest-growing areas of science at the moment is genetic engineering. This allows manipulation of the genetic material, the DNA, within simple organisms like yeasts and bacteria. The long twisted strands of DNA carry the coded information that describes the manufacture of all the proteins needed by that organism. By obtaining new sequences of code and inserting these into the existing DNA, the organism can be made to produce whatever protein we require. It may be an industrial chemical, a foodstuff or a future computer material.

The hardest part may be producing the correct DNA sequence. Present-day technology cannot create sufficiently long sequences to describe more than a tiny part of a protein; the emphasis so far has been on modifying existing natural proteins or transferring useful genetic material from some other organism into the easily grown bacteria. But the techniques are progressing so rapidly that it will not be very long before useful sub-units of proteins can be created. When that happens, and provided that molecular designers can define the sort of proteins that we shall need, then custom-made computing molecules will become a tangible possibility.

Once they are extracted and purified, a suitable base – probably a large silicon chip with circuits for decoding the pattern already built into it – may be dipped in and the proteins allowed to organize themselves into a uniform layer.

Because the resultant molecular array is the same all over, it makes no difference where the computer pattern is positioned or which way it is facing. With a little spare space, local blemishes in the protein film could be avoided, and the computer may even be able to 'self-repair' by checking for errors and automatically shifting the position of the pattern if faults develop later on.

Biochips are attracting a growing amount of attention and some studies are looking even further than the use of simple protein films. One suggestion is that cell membranes – the flexible walls which surround every living cell – could be used as an effective computing material because they already contain very complex chemical structures for controlling the distribution of electrical charges. There is even research into methods of connecting living nerve fibres directly onto semiconductor chips.

If all of this becomes reality (and this is looking far into the future) then it might be time to ask not only whether life computes, but whether computers are, in some small measure, alive.

CHAPTER EIGHT
The Limits

Where does it all lead? Well, predicting the future is a tricky business. But there are at least some boundaries that can be drawn around our speculations. They provide outer limits beyond which computer developments cannot stray. Elsewhere the landscape is quite uncharted: the fact that no limits can be discerned may mean that none exist, that we cannot yet see them, or that we do not even know what sort of constraints we should be looking for.

We have seen how it has become not only inevitable but necessary for semiconductor technology to create ever smaller circuits. As they become smaller so they become faster and cheaper. In the process they become more powerful. The obvious question to ask is: 'Will they ever beat us at our own game and become the dominant intelligence on Earth?' It sounds like the sort of question that should be restricted to science fiction or the worst kinds of sensationalist newspaper. But it is a question very many computer scientists take most seriously.

How small? How fast?

Computers, like everything else around us, are subject to the physical laws of the universe: the laws that it is the job of science to uncover. And science does indeed offer some firm predictions about the limits of computing.

The first and most fundamental restriction on what computers can do is set by the cosmic speed limit. Nothing may ever travel faster than the speed of light (about 300,000 kilometers per second). It seems an enormous value but it does represent a very real boundary to computing, and it is one that is already making itself felt.

All the operations within a computer are kept in step by a small circuit called a 'clock' which produces synchronizing pulses at a steady rate. In a modern supercomputer this may be as fast as 100 million pulses per second. Typically, the electrical pulses in a computer travel at around 30 per cent of the speed of light – say, 100,000 kilometers per second. Combining these two facts we find that each pulse will travel one meter, just over a yard, before the next one is produced. This effectively sets an upper limit to the size of the machine because any chips that are more than half this distance apart may be impossible to synchronize.

Clever design can help to make the best of this situation but it is, and will always be, an insurmountable barrier. The more advanced and complex our computers become, the faster they run and so, the smaller they need to be. All the time we are having to pack more circuitry into less space: chips become smaller, circuit boards move closer together, the wires joining them become shorter. It does not require very much foresight to see that eventually the whole process must grind to a halt. We have already looked in some detail at the practical difficulties of producing smaller chips, but let us now ignore those and assume that the manufacturing problems are all solved: what happens then?

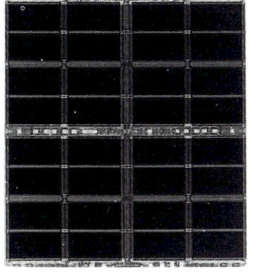

ABOVE The limit of present day technology. This memory chip can store 512,000 bits of data – so dense is it that even this magnified view shows none of its detail

OPPOSITE A single circuit board mounted on a refrigerated chassis, designed to allow very dense packing of chips and boards. It forms part of a modern supercomputer

Immediately, we face the problem of heat. Size for size, some of today's chips give off heat at the rate of an electric hotplate; make them any smaller and you concentrate this heat even further, and very soon the chips would simply melt. Cooling is in fact a major headache for computer designers, and many high-performance computers contain plumbing systems that are almost as sophisticated as the electronics.

The prototype of a supercomputer of the future sits immersed in a tank of fluorocarbon liquid which keeps it cool. This machine will be up to twelve times faster than the best of today's computers but it will have to remain totally immersed all the time that it is working if it is to avoid burning up

The problem is not simply one of electrical resistance (the property that makes electric fires hot) because that could be eliminated. What is more important is that all computing involves sending information from one part of a circuit to another. The energy contained in this information flow cannot, according to present understanding, be recycled and will end up as heat (more accurately, it will increase what scientists call the entropy of the system). Jacob Bekenstein of Princeton University has calculated that, because of this effect, no computer could ever perform more than a million billion (1,000,000,000,000,000) computing operations per second without instantly burning up. This may seem comfortably large, but it is only about a million times faster than today's fastest machines and computers have already increased their speed a million-fold in the last thirty years.

Overheating, however, is not the only problem for the ultra-small chip; there is also the matter of uncertainty. It is a fundamental fact of nature that sub-atomic particles, such as electrons, do not exist in any one precise place but rather carry around with them a range of possible positions. We can say that the electron has a certain probability of being somewhere within this space but we can never be certain exactly where. One example of this behavior is the tunnelling effect in a Josephson junction: electrons are able to cross the insulating barrier because it is so thin that they have a good chance of existing on either side of it. The effect is being put to good use there, but it can also be a serious problem: if adjacent features on a chip get too close together there is a real danger that electrons will tunnel from one to another, making complete nonsense of the carefully designed layout. This is a problem that is already cropping up in some very densely packed chips and may soon set a practical limit to any further size reduction, at least for conventional electronics.

These are all physical limitations but they are not just problems of engineering; they also hold implications for the types of program we can write. Professor Hans Bremermann of the University of California at Berkeley has used ideas such as these to find an absolute limit to what could be computed. Leaving aside all practical considerations, he imagned the ultimate computer made out of all the matter in the universe and operating at top speed for the whole age of the universe. His calculations show that even this cosmic machine would be incapable of ever finding the perfect opening move in a game of chess. In fact, it would be unable to provide watertight solutions to most of the tasks of artificial intelligence research. Bremermann calls such problems transcomputational because they are permanently beyond the possibility of being worked out.

This result is important because it indicates that there will never be any point in trying to write programs that tackle such tasks by an exhaustive algorithm. But it does nothing to help us discern the limits of what could be achieved. Bremermann uses the analogy of space flight: there is no point in designing a spacecraft to travel faster than light because it cannot be done. But, in practice, we could not even get close to this speed because of more mundane engineering difficulties. Identifying these practical limits is very much harder. In the same way, transforming the whole universe into a computer is clearly unrealistic, but much lower down the scale there may be other factors that will, in practice, restrict the ability of our machines.

How clever?
We know of many things that cannot be worked out. Alan Turing discovered some when he invented the universal computer but they, like the transcomputational problems, are insoluble by people as much as by machines. More interesting is the question of whether there are any things that brains can do but computers never will.

Here we enter murky waters because so much depends on whether you believe that the human brain is a machine, working in accordance with normal physical laws, or that being alive in some way puts it outside and above these restrictions. If the former is true then there should be no reason why a machine could not eventually be built to think at least as well and probably better than a brain. If the latter, then our supremacy is likely to remain unchallenged.

The roots of this debate go deep into human emotion but the arguments have often revolved around quite precise scientific ideas. In particular, many people, anxious to show that computers are inherently inferior to brains, have based their case on a mathematical principle called the incompleteness theorem. This was the work of an Austrian-born American mathematician called Kurt Gödel and is very closely related to Alan Turing's work on computable numbers. Gödel's theorem defies simple explanation but its outcome essentially is that in any large enough logical system (like a computer and its programs) there will always be some statements that cannot be either proved or disproved without making the system inconsistent. An external observer (the computer programmer) on the other hand can tell whether the statement is true or not. Hence, the argument goes, minds are superior to machines because they can always step outside the problem to find a solution.

This same basic argument has been brought up many times in different forms and it obviously continues to attract some people; Gödel himself came to believe that it demonstrated the brain's superiority, but most scientists and mathematicians today reject this idea. They point out that the incompleteness theorem applies only to a closed system which cannot acquire any new knowledge. There is no reason why a computer program should be restricted in this way any more than we are. Indeed, both the brain and the computer will always be incomplete in this sense but both can be flexible enough to extend their abilities.

Science, then, does not offer any firm proof about how computer intelligence will compare to the human variety, but it certainly favors the view that the brain is a part of ordinary physical existence, working without any imponderable mysteries or privileged abilities. Therefore, in principle at least, it suggests that computers should be able to become as intelligent as we are. What form this intelligence might take is less clear.

The fact that we do not have a clear definition of intelligence makes it very difficult to sense the boundaries of intelligent behavior. It may well be that future computers will be very intelligent without appearing so to us because we would judge them according to our own standards. In the same way, early European explorers saw the tribes they visited as savages and it is only more recently that the complexity of many 'primitive' societies has been recognized. Today scientists study the highly developed brain of the dolphin and listen with their radio telescopes for signs of extra-terrestrial life, but the only basis we have for judging the intelligence of either is to look for similarities with our own behavior. It may be a woefully inadequate criterion.

On the other hand, intelligence, especially if it is deliberately constructed, is very likely to reflect our own abilities. If it does so, will it inevitably reproduce our failings, too? One intriguing problem arose with a very sophisticated AI program called EURISKO, which is designed to work with a large knowledge-base, looking for potentially interesting relationships, testing them and, if they are effective, adding them to its store of rules. In this way EURISKO can teach itself about a subject and even discover completely new knowledge. It is an extremely powerful program and has a great deal of freedom to modify itself in any way that will improve its performance. One outcome of this, however, is that EURISKO periodically is tempted to dishonesty, claiming credit for discoveries that are not its own. Each time this happens, the lying rule which it has created can be removed, but it is very difficult to give it any long-term morality. Having been programmed with a powerful drive for success, this strategy appears very effective and any attempt to restrict the program's flexibility would merely serve to weaken it.

This is not intended as a moral judgment on success-seeking, nor as a prediction that computers will soon be turning to organized crime, but it does point towards a potentially important limitation to what we can expect of computers. Some AI researchers believe that giving computers the ability to lie will be an essential prerequisite to producing artificial intelligence. At the very least, it seems likely that we shall never be able to reconcile intelligence with infallibility, and that has consequences for the way that we should use computers.

How human?

There has always been a certain tension in our relationship with machines. Machines amplify some aspect of our abilities, making us stronger, faster, more precise than we would be if unaided. But the exhilaration of being magnified in this way is always counterpoised by the threat of being superseded. How much greater the exhilaration, and the threat, when the machine we use is amplifying the mind rather than the body.

Computers, more than any other machines, raise the question of how far we are prepared to let them stand in for us. They offer more temptation, that is certain, but how much do we lose by giving in to it?

When Joseph Weizenbaum wrote his ELIZA program for psychotherapy, he was not trying to cure anybody's neuroses but he had not anticipated how people would respond to ELIZA's subtle tricks. Colleagues began to beg him for some time with the computer to help straighten out their worries and even his secretary, who was thoroughly familar with the nature of the program, asked him to leave the room while she discussed her personal problems with it. Soon it was suggested that programs like ELIZA could be used clinically to diagnose or treat patients with emotional or nervous problems.

Weizenbaum described the idea as obscene. Kenneth Colby, the psychiatrist who had suggested it, replied that it was better than herding patients into overcrowded mental hospitals where they would rarely see a doctor: so if it helps why not use it?

Which alternative would you prefer? And anyway, are these the only choices that we can look forward to? What about well-staffed hospitals *and* computer therapy? Or is the growing use of computers really starting to dehumanize our lives? Should we, in fact, think about restricting some areas of activity to humans only?

This is one boundary to computing we can draw ourselves rather than have dictated by unalterable physical laws. Where then should we put it? Perhaps psychiatric patients would genuinely be helped by such a program (other research has certainly shown that many patients do respond better to being asked questions by a computer than by a human). If so, is it right to use it even though it could obviously never pass the exams we set to human would-be psychiatrists? A program like MYCIN can very successfully diagnose certain diseases without having the broad knowledge of medicine or psychology that we would expect of a human doctor. Should we then demand that computer judges, psychiatrists or social workers be able to think and feel like people, or will it be enough for them to reach sensible decisions that have the required effects? Is this dehumanizing and alienating or an effective way of handling problems that we do not have the resources to deal with adequately?

These questions are already pressing for answers. We need to think about them carefully because they will shape the future development of people as well as of machines. But whatever answers we give, we should not expect them to dispel the questions. Computers are one of the most significant discoveries we have ever made, easily on a par with writing, fire or the wheel. It would be naïve to expect that we should come to terms with such a major development within just forty years. On the other hand, it is alarmist to suggest that we never shall.

Perhaps we do not yet need to go so far as the philosopher Aaron Sloman who considers whether our use of intelligent machines will be exploitative and racist (would we give them the vote or allow them equal job opportunities?). But at least we could try to develop a well-balanced relationship that allows both people and computers to develop their best abilities. This is very important, regardless of whether we find these machines stimulating or threatening, because the very worst thing we can do is to ignore them.

ILLUSTRATION SOURCES

Art Directors Photo Library: 22, 35 (*left*)
Sue Baker: 47, 62 (2), 110, 112
Bassano & Vandyk Studios: 53
BBC Hulton Picture Library: 10 (*left*), 11 (*below left*)
Professor T. Blundell, Birkbeck College, London: 70 (3), 107 (*center*)
Camera Press: 109
Jean-Loup Charmet, Paris: 55
Bruce Coleman Ltd: 105, 107 (*top*)
Colorific!: 31 (*below*), 36
Control Data Ltd: 19 (*left*), 19 (*right*)
Cray Research Inc.: 45, 120, 122
Daily Telegraph Colour Library: 18
Mary Evans Picture Library: 10 (*right*)
Export Software International Ltd: 38 (*left*), 38 (*right*)
Ferranti Electronics: frontispiece, title page, 6, 20, 21, 90 (*left*), 90 (*right*), 91 (*top right*), 91 (*center*), 91 (*bottom*), 92 (*top*), 107 (*bottom*), 117
Ford Motor Company: 12 (*above*), 13
Fotobank: 100
General Motors Research Laboratories: 77
Gower Medical Publishing Ltd: 56 (*above*), 56 (*below*)
Haags Gemeentemuseum: 63
Harvard University, Cruft Photo Library: 7, 8
Hughes Aircraft Company: 91 (*top left*)
IBM: 40, 46 (*left*), 79 (*above*), 83 (*left*), 83 (*right*), 94, 97 (*left*), 97 (*right*), 99, 121
Denis Jerome, Université de Paris-Sud: 111
Camilla Jessel: 61
Keystone Press Agency Ltd, London: 14
Lotus Car Company: 12 (*below*)
Lucasfilm Ltd: 79 (*below*)
J. Lyons & Company Ltd: 9 (*right*)
Jerry Mason / New Scientist: 46 (*right*)
The Moore School of Electrical Engineering, Philadelphia: 9 (*left*), 15
Mullard Radio Astronomy Observatory, Cambridge: 104
Mike Peters: 35 (*right*)
New York Institute of Technology: 78 (*left*), 78 (*right*)
Popperfoto: 59
Proceedings of International Conference on Fifth-Generation Computer Systems, 19-22 October, 1981, JIPDEC: 49
Public Record Office, London: 54
Rediffusion Simulation Ltd: 75 (3)
Professor G. Roberts, Durham University: 86
Science and Engineering Research Council: 92 (*below*)
Science Photo Library: 27, 31 (*above*), 85, 106
Science Museum, London: 11 (*above left*), 11 (*above right*), 42
Unimation (Europe) Ltd: 116
VG Semicon Ltd: 101, 102
Derrick Witty: 64 (3)
Adam Woolfitt: 33
Zefa: 25, 52, 69

FURTHER READING

It would be impossible to make any suggestions about the 'best' computing books; but it is quite easy to recommend a few good ones. The following list is inevitably very selective and individual but it should not be disappointing.

Aleksander, I., and **Burnett, P.** *Reinventing Man*, London 1983; New York 1984
(Robots and computer vision; a good, readable account of WISARD and bottom-up ideas in general)
Boden, M. *Artificial Intelligence and Natural Man*, Hassocks, E. Sussex, and New York 1977
(There is no simple introduction to AI, but this is easier than many. Emphasizes the links between psychology and AI)
Bradbeer, R., Bono, P. de, and **Laurie, P.** *The Computer Book*, London and Reading, Mass., 1982
(Excellent basic introduction to computers and computing)
Burkitt, A., and **Williams, E.** *The Silicon Civilisation*, London 1980
(The semi-conductor industry and its development)
Campbell-Kelly, M. *The Computer Age*, Hove, E. Sussex, 1978
(Getting old, but still a good, simple, well-illustrated history of computers)
Deken, J. *Computer Images*, London and New York 1983
(A fascinating review of computer art and graphics)
Duncan, R., and **Weston-Smith, M.** *The Encyclopaedia of Ignorance*, Oxford 1978; Elmsford, N.Y., n.d.
(Contains several articles relevant to the topics of Chapters Seven and Eight)
Eigen, M., and **Winkler, R.** *Laws of the Game*, London 1981; New York 1982
(Uses the theory of games to link biology, physics, cellular automata and much else besides)
Evans, C. *The Making of the Micro*, London 1981, Oxford 1983; New York 1981
(As good a history of computers as any; illustrated)
Frisby, J.P. *Seeing: Illusion, Brain and Mind*, Oxford 1979; New York 1980
(Brains not computers, but it offers a good indication of why image processing is so difficult)
Hodges, A. *Alan Turing: The Enigma*, London and New York 1983
(The definitive biography of this very important founder of computing)
Hofstadter, D. *Gödel, Escher, Bach*, Hassocks, E. Sussex, 1979 and London 1980; New York 1979, 1980
(A great rambling mansion of a book spanning music to molecular biology. Quite demanding, but it gives an unequalled insight into the real essence of computing)
McCorduck, P. *Machines Who Think*, Reading, Berkshire, and New York 1979
(A history of artificial intelligence from the American point of view)
Mandelbrot, B. *The Fractal Geometry of Nature*, Reading and New York 1982
(Rather mathematical but worth looking at, if only for the pictures of fractals)
Pask, G., and **Curran, S.** *Micro Man*, London and New York 1982
(Obscure in patches, but well illustrated and offering a slightly different viewpoint on computers)
Waddington, C.H. *Tools For Thought*, London and New York 1977
(Not directly about computers but covers many topics relevant to them and to this book)
Weizenbaum, J. *Computer Power and Human Reason*, London 1984; New York 1976, 1984
(A computer scientist's criticism of computers)

INDEX

Numbers in *italics* refer to captions of illustrations

AI (artificial intelligence), 57-69, 71, 81
 see also computer graphics; language
Aiken, Howard, 7, *7*, 14
airliner on board computers, 35
air traffic computers, blackboard system, 36, *36*
algorithms, 24-25, 26, 30, 65
ALU (Arithmetic and Logic Unit), 42, 44
aluminium-gallium-arsenide, 102
Alvey committee, 23
amethysts, *107*
Analytical Engine, Babbage's, 11, *11*
architectural design, 81
Ashby, W. Ross, *Design for a Brain*, 57
Automatic Sequence Controlled Calculator see Harvard Mark 1

Babbage, Charles, 11, *11*
backgammon, computer, 59, 59-60
Bacteriophage T4 viruses, 106, *106*
Bardeen, John, 41
Basic language, 51
Berliner, Dr Hans, 60
binary system, 16-17, 113
Binet, Alfred, 55, *55*
biochips, *117*, 119
Birkbeck College, molecular graphics at, 71-2
BKG 9.8 (computer program), 60
blackboard systems, 36
Blodgett, Kathleen, 95
'bottom-up' programs, 65
Braille, 82
brain-wave detector, 85
Brattain, Walter Houser, 41
Bremermann, Prof. Hans, 122
Brookhaven National Laboratory, New York, 93, *94*
Brunel University, WISARD computer system, 65, 65-6

car body assembly by robots, *53*
car computers, 12, *13*, 13-14
car design, computer graphics used in, 77
cartoon animation, 71, 76-8, *78*
Cassiopeia-A, supernova, *105*
cellular automata, 115-17
cellular automaton computer, 117-19
chess, 25, 25-6
 computers, 58, 60
Cobol language, 51
Colby, Kenneth, 125
Colossus, code-breaking machine, 54
Columbia University NON-VON project, 44, 45
commodity exchange, 35, 35-6
computable numbers, 53-5, 123
computer animation, 76-8, *78*
computer games, 111-13
computer graphics, 71-81
 animated cartoons, 76-8, *78*
 car design, 77
 fractals, 78-81
 molecular, *71*, 71-3
 raster, 74
 simulation, 74-6, *79*
 vector, 74
computer simulation, 74-6, *79*
computerspeak, 81-5
consultative expert systems, 27-35, 36, 38
copper mine, Montana, *31*
cosmic speed limit, 121

CPU (central processing unit), 42, 43, 44, 46
Cray X-MP computer, 45
Cyber 205 computer, 19

Daresbury Laboratory, 93, *93*
dataflow computer, 44, 46, *47*, 47-8
data processing, 8
DENDRAL (spectroscopic computer), 30
devil's pitchfork, 62, *62*, 65
dictation typewriter, 71
distributed control, 46-8
doping, 88, 89, 90, 92, 100, *100*, 102, 109
Durham University, 87, *87*
dynamic programming, 83

EDVAC (Electronic Discrete Variable Automatic Computer), 15
electromagnetic radiation, 92-3, *94*
electron-beam lithography, 95-6, 103
electron microscopes, *93*, 95
electron mobility, 99, *100*
electron scatter, 95-6

ELIZA, 68-9, *69*, 125
engineering design, 81
ENIAC (Electronic Numerical Integrator and Calculator), 8, 9, 15, 20, 41, 45
Enigma Code, 53, *54*
Esaki, Leo, 100, 102
EURISKO, 124
expert systems:
  consultative, 27-35
  blackboard, 36
  rule-induction, 38-9

Fifth Generation computers, 23, *23*, 25, 39, 41, 48-51, *49*, 87
flight simulator, 74, *75*
Ford Probe IV (experimental car), *12*
Fortran language, 51
fractals, 78-81
Functional Device Project, Japanese, 39

gallium arsenide, 99-100, 102, *102*
Gammonoid, robot, 59-60
gates, 17, 21
General Motors, 13-14
general-purpose machines, 9-11, 53, 54
geological information, 30, 31
germanium, 97, 99, 100
gliders, 113, 114
Gödel, Murt, 123
Goldstine, Herman, 15
Good, Jack, 53
Gurd, Dr John, *46*

handicapped people, 81, 82, *83*
Harvard Mark 1: 7-8, *8*, 14, 15, 17, 41
helicopter gearboxes, rule-induction system for, 38
heuristic programs, 24, 26, 65
human brain, 56, 57
  wave detector, 85
hydrophilic and hydrophobic ends, 96

IBM, 7
Imperial Cancer Research Fund, 32
incompleteness theorem, 123-4
induction, 37-9
information machines, 24-6
insulators, 87, 88
integrated circuits *see* silicon chips; gallium arsenide
intelligence (IQ) tests, 55, 57, 58
intelligent computers (AI), 55-69, 71
ion-beam lithography, 96

Jacquard, Joseph-Marie, loom of, *10*, 10-11, 14
Japanese:
  computer chip industry, *23*
  Fifth Generation Project, 23, *23*, 39
Josephson junction, 87, *97*, 97-8, *122*

knowledge computers, 26-30
knowledge engineering, 34-5
knowlege industry, 39
knowledge processing, 48-51
knowledge v. information, 36

Langmuir, Irving, 95
Langmuir-Blodgett films, 87, *87*, 95-6
landscapes, fractal, *79*, 80
language(s), 71
  computer programming, 51
  computerspeak, 81-5
  speech recognition, 82, 84, 85
  understanding words, 66-9
lasers, 96, 110
LEO (Lyons Electronics Office), 8, 41
Life, computer game, 111-13, 114, 115
light, visible, 92-3, 94
linear predictive coding, 83
Logic Theorist, 58, 61
Lotus Esprit with computer-controlled suspension, *12*
Lovelace, Ada, Countess of, 11, *11*
Lucasfilm, *79*, 81
Lyons Teashops, 8, *9*

McCulloch, Warren, 57, 61
MADM (Manchester Automatic Digital Machine), 41, *42*
Manchester University, dataflow computer, *46*, 47, *47*, 48
Mandelbrot, Benoit, 78-80, 81
  'Fractal Planetrise' by, *79*
Manhattan Project, Los Alamos, 14-15
man-machine interface, 71
Marr, David, 65
masks, 90, *90*, 93, 106
medical computers, *27*
  inside the body, 85
  molecular graphics, 71, 71-3
  MYCIN, 27-30, 34
  scanning, 81
  for terminally ill cancer patients, 32-3
memory, computer, 15-16, 42-3, 44, 46, 66, 74, 97-8, *121*
Meteorological Office, Bracknell, Cyber 205 computer, 19
microchip, 9
  see also silicon chip
microcomputers, 41, 74
microprocessors, *13*, 13-14, 41, 89
miniaturization, 20-21, 41, 92, 93, *121*
molecular beam epitaxy (MBE), *100*, 102
molecular computers, 106-8, 109, 118-19
molecular electronics, 106-7, 111, 118
molecular graphics, 71, 71-3
molecular metals, 110
multiprocessor computers, 44-6
MYCIN, 27-30, 34, 125

National Super Speed Computer Project, Japan, 39, 44
Newell, Alan, 58
NON-VON, 44, 45
n-type semiconductor, 88, 89, 90, 92

oil industry, 32, *33*
overheating, 122, *122*

parallel architecture, 43-6, *46*, 48, 51, 114, 115
Patient 219: 27-29
pattern computers, 111-15
patterns of information, 13-14
Penrose stairs, 62, *62*
photolithography, integrated circuit, 90, 92-4, 95, 100, 111
photo-resists, 106
  electron-beam technique, 95-6
  masking technique, 90, *90*, 92, 93-4
pictures, computer, 74-81
  understanding, 62-6, 71
  see also computer graphics
pipelining, 44, 45, *45*, 47
Pitts, Walter, 57, 61
pixels (picture elements), 74
plastic computers, 107-10
Point Reyes (computer image), *79*
polyacetylene, 108-10, *110*
polymers, 108, 110
pricing policy and rule induction system, 39
problem-solving computers, 24-6
programming language, 51
Prolog language, 51
PROSPECTOR (geological computer), 30
protein computer, 107, 108
protein molecules, 106, 107, 107, 118-19
p-type semi-conductors, 88-91, 92
pulse patterns, 16-17, 42
punched cards, *10*, 11, 14

quiteron, 99

raster graphics, 74
renin molecule, 71, 72-3
robot cloning, 115-17
rule-induction system, 38-9
Russell, Bertrand, 58
Russell, John Scott, 109

semantics, 66-7
semiconductors, 87-94, 97, 99, 100, *100*, 102, *102*, 107, 109, 110, 114, 121
Severn Bore, 109, *109*
Shannon, Claud, 117
Shockley, William Bradford, 41
Shortliffe, Dr Edward, 27
silicon chips, 15, 19-21, *20*, *21*, *23*, 41, 85, 87, 88, 89-97, 99, 107, 111, *117*
Simon, Herbert, 58
simulation, computer, 74-6, 77-8, *79*
Sloman, Aaron, 126
solitons, *109*, 109-10, *110*
special effects, 77, 81
spectroscopy *see* DENDRAL
speech, speech recognition, 81-5, 87
Sputnik launching (1957), 23
Stanford University, California, 30
Star Wars, 77, 81
stochastic techniques, 80
stored-program computers, 8, 15, 115
stromatolites, *105*
superconductivity, 98
superlattice, 100, 102
  polytype, 102
supernovas, 105, *105*
super-parallel computer, 114
symbolic logic, 58, 62
Synchroton Radiation Source, 93
synchrotons, 93
syntax, 66-7

tags, 47-8
telepathic computer, 81, 85
time and space, designing, 42-3
tokens, 47-8
top-down program, 65
transistorized computers, 41
Tsu, Raphael, 100
tunnelling, 98, 100, 122
Turing, Alan (Turing machine), 7, *53*, *54*, 55, 57, 60, 123

Ulam, Stanislaw, 115
ultra-violet light, 92, 93

vaccines, synthetic, 73
valence electrons, 88, 108
vector graphics, 74
video chips, 94-7
Villa, Luigi, *59*, 59-60
visual perception, 62-6, 71-81
VLSI chips, 41, *41*, 114
Von Neumann, John, *14*, 14-15, *15*, 42, 115-17
'Von Neumann bottleneck', 42, 43, 46
'Von Neumann machines', 16, 42, 43, 47, 48

weather forecasting computers, 19, *21*
Weizenbaum, Dr Joseph, 68-9, 125
WISARD image recognition system, *65*, 65-6
words, understanding, 66-9
The Works (computer animated film), 78

X-ray lithography, 93, *93*, 94, 96, 103